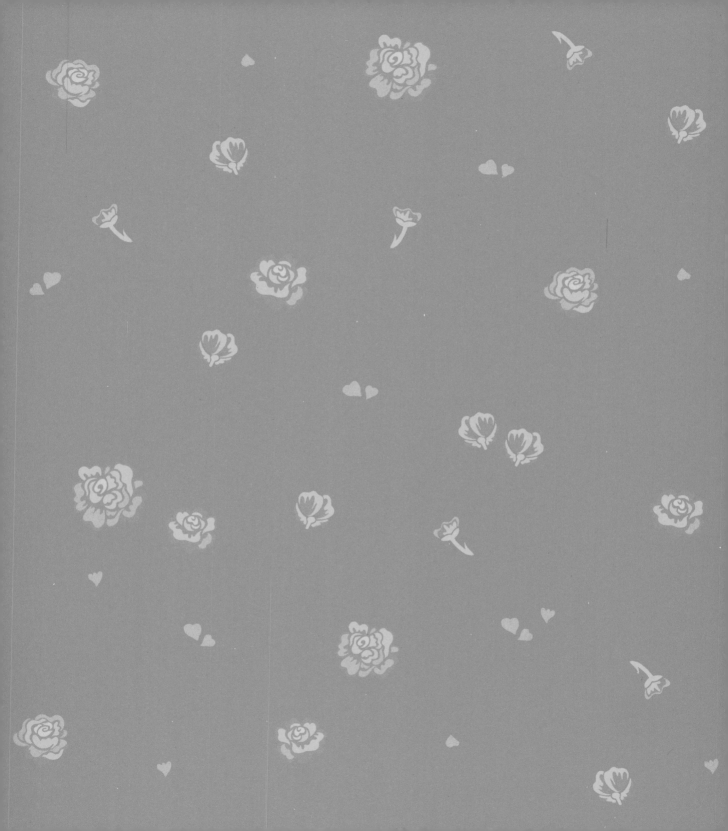

Betty Crocker™

Found Recipes

Betty Crocker™

Found Recipes

Beloved Vintage Recipes
Worth Sharing

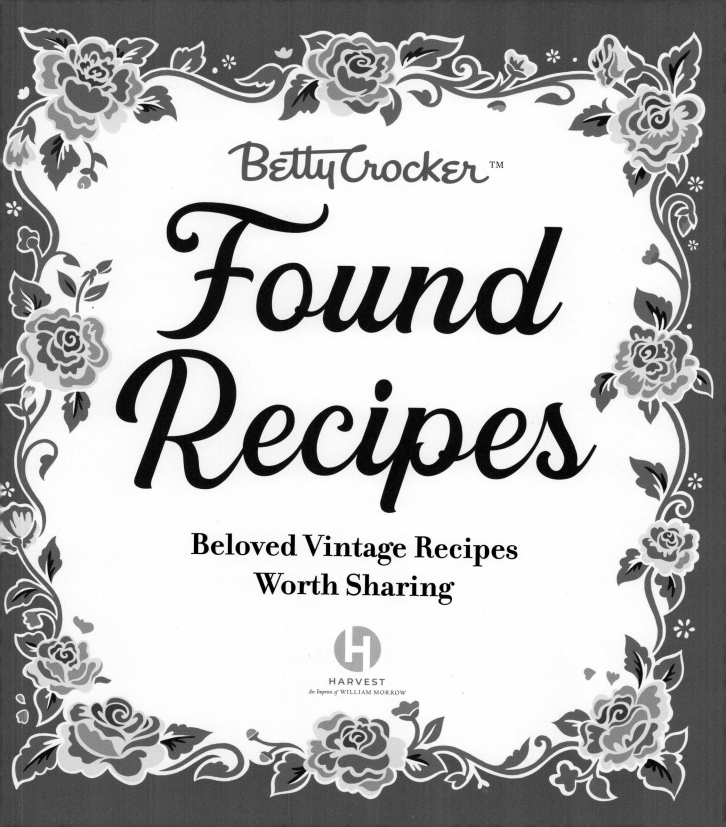

HARVEST

An Imprint of WILLIAM MORROW

GENERAL MILLS

Director, Brand Experience Creative: Melissa Wildermuth

Manager, Brand Experience Creative: Kristin Roth

Executive Editor/Food Editor: Cathy Swanson Wheaton

Recipe Development and Testing: Betty Crocker Kitchens

Photography: General Mills Photography Studios and Tony Kubat Photography

Photographer: ReGina Murphy

Photo Assistant: Landen Nitz

Food Stylists: Carol Grones, Melinda Hutchinson, Betsy Nelson

Food Styling Assistant: Jerry Dudycha

Prop Stylist: Michele Joy

Inspiring America to Cook at Home™

HARVEST

Vice President and Editorial Director: Deb Brody

Senior Editor: Sarah Kwak

Assistant Editor: Jacqueline Quirk

Production Supervisor: Kimberly Kiefer

Managing Editor: Jennifer Eck

Production Editor: Hope Breeman

Interior Design: Tai Blanche

Cover Design: Yeon Kim

Share the joy of homemade with more yummy recipes and helpful cooking tips at BettyCrocker.com

Letter from the Editors

Dear Friends,

We've dusted off our old cookbooks and dug through our archives to bring together some of the favorite recipes of our past that deserve a seat at today's table. There are so many wonderful recipes that have been created over our 100+ year history . . . which ones were the right ones to grace the pages of this special book?

We asked consumers for those recipes from their past that triggered fond memories. We worked with our Customer Care Team to find the recipes they were getting requests for. You'll see the best of these found recipes tagged throughout the book. And, for this specially curated collection, we also chose those recipes that had risen to the top of *our* recipe boxes over the years, because when you work in the Betty Crocker Test Kitchens, you taste *hundreds* of recipes! These recipes might either spark a memory of yours, or become a new one for you and those you lovingly prepare them for.

During our search, our fans told us about favorite recipes they'd lost, but that we couldn't find. We knew we had to get into the kitchen and take a whisk! From what our fans remembered about the recipes, we re-created them with delicious results. Look for these re-created lost recipes and their memories behind them inside.

I've been empowering cooks to be successful in the kitchen for generations, because gathering people and the connections that can be made over good food is evergreen. Enjoy my story and the history in the baking behind more than a century of encouraging makers of all skill levels, gender, or age to be Bettys, too.

XOXO,

Betty

Contents

Introduction: The Betty Crocker Story   ix

Holiday Celebrations   1

Memorable Main Dishes   49

Warm from the Oven Breads   111

Irresistible Cookies & Bars   157

Better Than Ever Desserts   199

Metric Conversion Guide   253

Index   254

March 15, 1944

Mrs. J. Armendarez, Jr.
3608 Folsom St.
Los Angeles, 33, Calif.

My dear Mrs. Armendarez:

You are registered as a member of the Radio
Cooking School for the fall, winter and spring
terms and I'm delighted to have you with us as
a member.

How nice to hear that you have enjoyed using
our products and recipes and hearing our programs for so long a time!   I know what a
thrill it must be to have such fine results
with your bakings, especially when you receive
such nice compliments from your family and I
can assure you that you will always have the
same fine baking results as long as you continue to use our products and recipes together.

That was such a cute story that you told about
your young daughter and what she thinks of our
recipes.   Thank you for telling me about it
and for recommending our flour and recipes to
your friends and relatives.

Under separate cover I am sending you a copy
of our Lunch Box bulletin with additional
suggestions for interesting sandwich spreads.

Hoping this material will be helpful and again
thanking you for all your very kind, appreciative
comments,

                              Cordially,

BC: JHs

Consumer letter from Betty Crocker, 1944.

Introduction

The Betty Crocker Story

No . . . she's not a real person . . . but she's baked her way into the hearts of cooks for more than 100 years, creating products and recipes that people love. The first lady of food, she's set the standard for well-tested recipes and reliable products, adapting with the times while staying grounded to the past, to become the global icon (and trusty friend in the kitchen) she is today.

With great-tasting products spanning grocery store shelves across the globe, sharing recipes, tips, and tricks through one of the most popular cooking websites, bettycrocker.com, and nearly 300 cookbook titles under our belt, Betty Crocker is still leveling the playing field for all makers today; innovating new ways to make food simple, inspirational, and achievable. Her superpower remains deliciously the same: spreading the joy of homemade cooking and baking and the love it creates for connections and deepening relationships with families, friends, and communities.

How Betty Was "Born"

A simple advertisement in the *Saturday Evening Post* in 1921 was destined to bake up a masterpiece. The ad for Gold Medal™ flour from our predecessor company, the Washburn Crosby Company, asked consumers to complete a picture puzzle to receive a small Gold Medal flour sack pin cushion. With more than 30,000 puzzles sent in came several hundred letters asking a variety of cooking and baking questions.

Thinking outside the recipe box, executives created a female personality within the home services department to reply to the letters. The warm and friendly name "Betty" was chosen for its popularity at the time. "Crocker" was selected as the surname to honor a recently retired director.

What's Cooking, Betty?

As many as 5,000 consumer letters a day were received. Not only did the staff answer their cooking questions, they also dispensed advice about everything else women as well as men asked about: entertaining, tips, maintaining a home, and even how to get along with an unhelpful husband. Betty also politely declined the multitude of wedding proposals she would receive each week, being that "she was married to her work!"

Betty's Signature

Betty Crocker

An informal contest was held among female employees to find the most distinctive Betty Crocker signature. It remains the basis of the Betty Crocker logo of today.

Betty Gets Her Red On

No official portraits of Betty existed until she was 15. A prominent commercial artist was commissioned to create the 1936 portrait, using various facial features of women working in the home services department. Her classic red jacket and white collar established a tradition that all seven future portraits followed.

Over the years, her look has been influenced by popular women of the times, including her hair style and clothing. We love how she's gotten younger with age . . . but we're perplexed by her changing eye color . . . contacts perhaps?

The Red Spoon Promise

In 1954, it became clear that putting Betty's face on packages wasn't realistic. A symbol was needed for what Betty Crocker stood for: "kitchen helper," "warm and friendly," and "reliable guide." A red spoon with her signature became an easily recognized Betty Crocker brand symbol for quality ever since.

Cooking Across the Radio Waves

In 1924, *Gold Medal Flour Home Service Talks* began on the Washburn Crosby Company's radio station in Minnesota. Soon after, the nation's first consumer food service program . . . the Betty Crocker *Cooking School of the Air* came into people's living rooms across the country. Recipes were shared, baking ideas and household tips were offered by the voice of "Betty Crocker." The cooking school continued without interruption for 24 years, attracting more than 1 million formal registrants. It still holds the record as one of the longest-running national radio programs of any kind in radio history.

Homemakers of Tomorrow

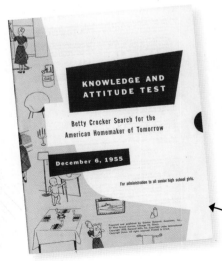

From 1955 to 1977, the Betty Crocker Search for the All-American Homemaker of Tomorrow program had more than 9.5 million high school seniors participate by taking a test about all things related to home management to earn the distinction. More than $2.1 million in scholarships were awarded for higher education.

1955 Betty Crocker Search for the American Homemaker of Tomorrow test.

Come into Our Kitchens

When General Mills opened its new headquarters in Golden Valley, Minnesota, it began a daily tour schedule of the Betty Crocker Kitchens. Invitations were sent, inviting people to "come into our kitchens and see where we test and develop new recipes, work on new products, and perfect quicker, easier methods to help you in your homemaking."

Nearly 2 million people visited the Betty Crocker Kitchens from 1958 to 1985, making it one of the state's top tourist attractions. From elementary school students to politicians and celebrities, people came to peek where Betty Crocker whipped up her famous recipes. In 1985, the tour program was closed to the public to preserve the confidentiality of its new product development and testing.

She's Still Mixing It Up

The publication in 1950 of *The Betty Crocker Picture Cook Book* marked the first cookbook of its kind, showing images of how to make the recipes. Over the years and now 13 editions later, more than 75 million copies of this cookbook, affectionately called "Big Red," have been sold. Each edition is a like a time capsule, containing both the tried-and-true favorites . . . and trending, contemporary recipes of the era.

BAKED ALASKA
A dessert of beauty . . . and mystery.

Blushing Apple Pies, from the *Betty Crocker Cookbook*, 13th Edition.

Baked Alaska, from *The Betty Crocker Picture Cook Book* (1950).

Betty's Got Your Back

"Betty . . . I need a recipe for . . ." It's Betty's favorite phrase, ever! Bettycrocker.com lets cooks of any skill set be whisk takers, batter makers, and savvy bakers. From our test kitchens to yours, only the highest quality, most reliably tasty, and intuitive kitchen solutions deserve the Betty name.

The site offers both scratch and product-based recipes for all occasions with the best tips and tricks for sweet success, meal planning, and money-saving ideas, and even coupons. Our "Ask Betty" feature covers the basic questions makers have, and you can even get answers to your burning questions (hopefully, nothing is *really* burning). No matter what kind of inspiration, recipe need, or cooking question you have, Betty's got your back!

Recipe Testing

- Large eggs and 2% milk were used unless otherwise indicated.
- Fat-free, low-fat, low-sodium, or lite products were not used unless indicated.
- No nonstick cookware and bakeware was used unless otherwise indicated. No dark-colored, black, or insulated bakeware was used.
- When a "pan" is called for, that means a metal pan was used; a baking "dish" or pie plate means ovenproof glass was used.
- An electric hand mixer was used for mixing only when mixer speeds are specified.

Calculating Nutrition

- The first ingredient was used wherever a choice is given, such as ⅓ cup sour cream or plain yogurt.
- The first amount was used whenever a range is given, such as a 3- to 3½-pound whole chicken.
- The first serving number was used whenever a range is given, such as 4 to 6 servings.
- "If desired" ingredients were not included.
- Only the amount of a marinade or frying oil that is absorbed was included.

Holiday Celebrations

Cheese balls were all the rage in the '50s through the '70s. What a yummy way to serve cheese and crackers—the ingredient combo makes it irresistible! It's a smart choice for entertaining, as it can be made in advance.

Pineapple Cheese Ball

Prep Time: 10 Minutes
Start to Finish: 1 Hour
   10 Minutes
12 servings (2 tablespoons each)

¼ cup finely chopped green
   bell pepper

¼ cup shredded carrot
1 package (8 oz) cream cheese
   or ⅓-less-fat cream cheese
   (Neufchâtel), softened
1 can (8 oz) crushed pineapple
   in juice, drained

½ cup unsalted roasted
   sunflower seeds or
   chopped nuts
Crackers, melba toast,
   or fresh veggies, if desired

1 In medium bowl, mix bell pepper, carrot, cream cheese, and pineapple. Cover and refrigerate for 1 hour or until mixture is firm enough to shape into a ball.

2 On plastic wrap or waxed paper, form mixture into a ball; roll in sunflower seeds. Cover and refrigerate until serving time. Serve with crackers.

1 Serving Calories 110; Total Fat 10g (Saturated Fat 4g, Trans Fat 0g); Cholesterol 20mg; Sodium 60mg; Total Carbohydrate 4g (Dietary Fiber 0g); Protein 2g **Carbohydrate Choices:** 0

Hors d'Oeuvres

Olive-and-Bacon	.50	Garlic Olives	.50
Wrapped Sweet Pickles	.50	Green Balls	.50
Cornucopias	.50	Burning Bush	.50
Dried Beef Rolls	.50	Triple Treat	.50
Wedgies	.50	Savory Dill Franks	.50

COLORFUL RELISHES FOR DECORATING
APPETIZER TRAY

Attractive relishes and garnishes that give colorful appeal to the Appetizer Tray are: radish roses or accordions, celery curls, tomato flowers, bouquets of parsley, carrot or turnip lilies, etc. Stuffed Cucumber, Celery Trunks, and Stuffed Celery are interesting additions.

STUFFED CUCUMBER

Remove center from pared cucumber with apple corer. Stuff tightly with a firm cheese mixture. Chill and slice ¼" thick.

CELERY TRUNKS

Fill matching stalks of celery with well seasoned cream cheese. Then fit the stalks back together (the way they were grown). Tie with string and chill. When firm, slice ½" thick. The celery curls around the cheese in attractive form.

STUFFED CELERY

Fill stalks with Roquefort cheese softened with cream cheese and seasoned with a drop or two of Worcestershire sauce. Or fill with a mixture of 1 cup mashed avocado, 2 tbsp. grated horseradish, and ½ tsp. tabasco sauce. Sprinkle with paprika. Chill.

All you have to do—

"To have a delicious appetizer on hand for holiday entertaining," says Valentine Thorson, longtime friend and Director of Home Service, Northern States Power Company, Minneapolis, "make a Green Cheese Ball. It's so easy!"

GREEN CHEESE BALL

Soften equal amounts of sharp American, white cream, and Roquefort type cheese. Season well. Mix in chopped pecans and minced parsley. Form into a large ball. Roll in minced parsley and chopped nuts.

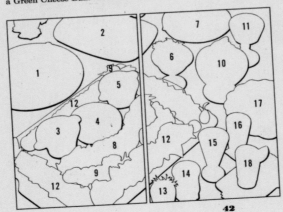

Where to find recipes for Appetizers in color photograph, pp. 44 and 45:

1. Plate of Canapés	.48,	49
2. Platter of Hors d'Oeuvres		50
3. Roquefort Spread		49
4. Cocktail Sauce		46
5. Cheese, Olive, Anchovy Spread		49
6. Crabmeat Cocktail		46
7. Fruit Plate		49
8. Fresh Cooked Shrimp		46
9. Celery Trunks and Other Relishes		42
10. Shrimp Cocktail		46
11. Fruit Cup		47
12. Simple Accompaniments		47
13. Cranberry Cocktail		46
14. Frozen Fruit Cocktail		47
15. Tomato Juice		47
16. Vegetable Juice Cocktail		46
17. Fresh Strawberry Plate		47
18. Fruit Juice Cocktail		47

42

A page from the Betty Crocker 1950 cookbook, including a recipe for Green Cheese Ball.

This flavorful dip was originally created in the 1920s by the chef at the Palace Hotel in San Francisco, for an actor who was appearing in a local play of the same name. Choose whatever veggies you like to serve with it; use it as a salad dressing or as a sauce for fish or shellfish.

Green Goddess Dip

Prep Time: 10 Minutes
Start to Finish: 8 Hours 10 Minutes
2 cups

¾ cup sour cream
¾ cup mayonnaise or salad dressing

¼ cup chopped fresh parsley
3 tablespoons chopped fresh chives
1 tablespoon tarragon vinegar or cider vinegar
¼ teaspoon salt
⅛ teaspoon pepper

2 medium green onions, finely chopped (2 tablespoons)
1 clove garlic, finely chopped
1 can (2 oz) anchovy fillets in pure olive oil, drained, finely chopped
Cut-up fresh vegetables, if desired

1 In medium bowl, mix all ingredients except fresh vegetables. Cover and refrigerate at least 8 hours but no longer than 3 days to blend flavors.

2 Serve with vegetables.

2 Tablespoons Calories 100; Total Fat 10g (Saturated Fat 2.5g, Trans Fat 0g); Cholesterol 15mg; Sodium 200mg; Total Carbohydrate 0g (Dietary Fiber 0g); Protein 1g **Carbohydrate Choices:** 0

From Betty Crocker's 1988 *Holiday Snacks* magazine, this clever way to serve chicken salad spread gave people four ways to enjoy it in just one recipe. With today's love of boards and charcuterie trays, we thought this should make a comeback. It's a charcuterie tray all on its own!

Chicken Salad Log

Prep Time: 20 Minutes
Start to Finish: 4 Hours
   20 Minutes

4 cups

CHICKEN SALAD

1 package (8 oz) cream cheese
   or ⅓-less-fat cream cheese
   (Neufchâtel), softened

¼ cup mayonnaise or salad
   dressing

2 tablespoons fresh lemon juice

½ teaspoon salt

¼ teaspoon ground ginger

⅛ teaspoon pepper

4 drops red pepper sauce

2 cups cut-up cooked chicken

2 hard-cooked eggs, chopped

4 medium green onions,
   sliced (¼ cup)

TOPPINGS

3 tablespoons chopped pitted
   ripe olives

3 tablespoons chopped green
   onions or green bell pepper

1 tablespoon toasted
   sesame seed

3 tablespoons diced pimiento
   (from 4-oz jar), drained

Assorted crackers or slices of
   baguette and cut-up fresh
   veggies, if desired

1 In medium bowl, mix cream cheese, mayonnaise, lemon juice, salt, ginger, pepper, and pepper sauce until well blended. Stir in chicken, eggs, and green onions.

2 Place chicken mixture on plastic wrap; shape into a log, 8×2 inches. Wrap with plastic wrap and refrigerate for about 4 hours or until firm.

3 Sprinkle olives over one-fourth of log. Repeat with green onions, sesame seed, and pimiento. Serve with crackers and veggies.

2 Tablespoons Calories 60; Total Fat 5g (Saturated Fat 2g, Trans Fat 0g); Cholesterol 25mg; Sodium 90mg; Total Carbohydrate 0g (Dietary Fiber 0g); Protein 3g **Carbohydrate Choices:** 0

This recipe was lost in the Betty Crocker Kitchens library, from before our computer recipe database was created. We were so happy to find it in a dusty 1997 Bisquick™ cookbook between the stacks. Both the original orange and the blueberry-orange pancakes are very delicious—no wonder Laura's family enjoyed them often!

Blueberry-Orange Pancakes

Prep Time: 35 Minutes
Start to Finish: 35 Minutes
7 servings (2 pancakes and about 2 tablespoons sauce each)

SAUCE
¼ cup sugar
1½ teaspoons cornstarch

¼ teaspoon orange zest
2 tablespoons fresh orange juice
2 cups fresh or frozen blueberries

PANCAKES
2 cups Bisquick Original Pancake & Baking Mix

1 cup milk
2 eggs
1 teaspoon orange zest
¼ teaspoon ground nutmeg
1 cup fresh or frozen blueberries
Additional orange zest, if desired

1 In 1½-quart saucepan, mix sugar, cornstarch, orange zest, and orange juice until smooth. Stir in 2 cups blueberries. Heat to boiling over medium heat, stirring constantly. Boil uncovered for about 2 minutes, stirring occasionally, until thickened. Keep warm.

2 In medium bowl, stir together all pancake ingredients except 1 cup blueberries and additional orange zest until blended. Fold in blueberries.

3 Heat griddle or skillet over medium-high heat (375°F). To test griddle, sprinkle with a few drops of water. If bubbles jump around, heat is just right. Brush with vegetable oil if necessary.

4 For each pancake, pour slightly less than ¼ cup batter onto hot griddle. Cook for 2 to 3 minutes or until bubbly on top and dry around edges. Flip and cook other side until golden brown.

5 Top servings of pancakes with syrup and additional orange zest.

Orange Pancakes with Maple-Orange Syrup: Omit sauce. In pancake batter, substitute ½ cup fresh orange juice for ½ cup of the milk; omit nutmeg and blueberries. In 1-quart saucepan, heat ¾ cup maple-flavored syrup, 2 tablespoons each fresh orange juice and butter over medium heat, stirring occasionally, until hot. Serve with pancakes.

1 Serving Calories 240; Total Fat 3.5g (Saturated Fat 1.5g, Trans Fat 0g); Cholesterol 55mg; Sodium 360mg; Total Carbohydrate 45g (Dietary Fiber 2g); Protein 6g **Carbohydrate Choices:** 3

1931 Bisquick package made it possible to have biscuits oven-ready in 90 seconds.

Eventually
GOLD MEDAL
Why Not Now

BISQUICK

GOLD MEDAL "KITCHEN TESTED" FLOUR, VEGETABLE SHORTENING, PHOSPHATE, SUGAR, DRY SKIM MILK, SALT, SODA.

90 SECONDS FROM PACKAGE TO OVEN.

ALL READY!
ADD MILK OR WATER – *NOTHING ELSE*
to Bake Beautiful Biscuits
REG. U.S. PAT. OFF.   COPYRIGHT 1931 BY GENERAL MILLS, INC.

Fan Memory

"We enjoyed these at Saturday morning breakfast with the whole family. These were the best pancakes and syrup."

—Laura W.

This clever festive breakfast casserole appeared in our 1999 holiday magazine. Any recipe that's a breeze to put together, can be made ahead, and features the flavors of the season is a winner in our book!

Eggnog French Toast Strata with Cranberry Syrup

Prep Time: 15 Minutes
Start to Finish: 9 Hours
8 servings (1 square and about
    ¼ cup syrup each)

STRATA

1 loaf (1 lb) French bread, cut
    into ½-inch-thick slices

3 oz (from 8-oz package) cream
    cheese or ⅓-less-fat cream
    cheese (Neufchâtel), softened
2½ cups dairy eggnog
6 tablespoons butter, melted
8 eggs
¼ teaspoon ground nutmeg

CRANBERRY SYRUP

1 cup frozen cranberry
    raspberry juice concentrate
    (from 12-oz can), thawed
1 cup jellied cranberry sauce
    (from 14-oz can)
⅓ cup sugar

1 Grease 13×9-inch rectangular or oval (3-quart) baking dish with vegetable shortening or spray with cooking spray. Arrange enough bread slices to cover bottom of greased dish. Spread tops of bread slices in dish with cream cheese. Arrange remaining bread slices on top.

2 In large bowl, mix eggnog, butter, and eggs with whisk until well blended. Pour evenly over bread slices. With back of spoon, gently press bread into dish. Sprinkle with nutmeg. Cover with plastic wrap; refrigerate 8 hours or overnight.

3 Heat oven to 325°F.

4 Uncover dish. Bake 30 to 35 minutes or until center is set and edges are light golden brown. Let stand 10 minutes before cutting.

5 Meanwhile, in 1-quart saucepan, mix all syrup ingredients. Cook over medium-low heat, stirring constantly with whisk, until cranberry sauce and sugar have melted.

6 Cut strata into 2 rows by 4 rows. Serve with warm cranberry syrup.

1 Serving Calories 560; Total Fat 25g (Saturated Fat 13g, Trans Fat 0.5g); Cholesterol 260mg; Sodium 600mg; Total Carbohydrate 69g (Dietary Fiber 1g); Protein 16g **Carbohydrate Choices:** 4½

From the 1988 *Betty Crocker Christmas* cookbook, these crepes will steal the show at any holiday brunch. With the handy make-ahead directions below, you can serve these with ease.

Raspberry-Almond Crepes

Prep Time: 45 Minutes
Start to Finish: 45 Minutes
8 servings

FILLING
1 box (4-serving size) vanilla instant pudding and pie filling mix
2 cups half-and-half
½ teaspoon almond extract

SAUCE
3 tablespoons sugar
1 teaspoon cornstarch
⅓ cup water
1 package (10 oz) frozen raspberries, thawed

CREPES
1½ cups Gold Medal all-purpose flour
1 tablespoon sugar
½ teaspoon baking powder
½ teaspoon salt
2 cups milk
2 eggs
2 tablespoons butter, melted
½ teaspoon vanilla

Sliced almonds, if desired

1 In medium bowl, mix all filling ingredients with whisk; beat 2 minutes. Let stand at room temperature while preparing sauce and crepes.

2 In 1-quart saucepan, mix 3 tablespoons sugar and the cornstarch. Gradually stir in water and raspberries. Cook over low heat, stirring constantly, until mixture thickens and boils. Boil and stir 1 minute; remove from heat. Let stand uncovered at room temperature while preparing crepes.

3 In medium bowl, mix flour, 1 tablespoon sugar, baking powder, and salt. Stir in remaining crepe ingredients except almonds; beat with whisk until smooth.

4 Lightly butter 6-inch skillet, then heat over medium heat until bubbly. Pour scant ¼ cup batter into skillet; immediately rotate skillet until thin film covers bottom. Cook until bottom is light brown. Run wide spatula around edge to loosen; flip and cook other side until bottom is light brown. Place on heatproof plate. Cover to keep warm. Repeat with remaining batter, stacking crepes by placing waxed paper between them.

5 For each serving, spoon about 2 tablespoons of the pudding mixture down center of each of 2 crepes; roll up. Place crepes seam side down on serving plate. Repeat with remaining crepes and pudding mixture. Top each serving with about 2½ tablespoons warm sauce each; sprinkle with almonds.

Make-Ahead Directions: Crepes can be made and refrigerated up to 3 days ahead or frozen up to 3 months. Wrap stack of 6 to 8 crepes (with waxed paper in between them) with plastic wrap or foil. Refrigerate or freeze. When ready to use, thaw frozen crepes at room temperature 3 hours. Unwrap crepes (leaving waxed paper between crepes). Heat in microwave on High about 30 seconds or until warm.

1 Serving Calories 350; Total Fat 13g (Saturated Fat 7g, Trans Fat 0g); Cholesterol 80mg; Sodium 460mg; Total Carbohydrate 51g (Dietary Fiber 2g); Protein 8g **Carbohydrate Choices:** 3½

From our 1999 Christmas cookbook, you can't beat the flavor of homemade coffee cakes like this one. Wondering how you can make scratch pastries in time for breakfast? Follow our simple make-ahead directions below that allow you to start the coffee cakes the day ahead and then bake them up fresh for breakfast the next day!

Raspberry and Cream Cheese Coffee Rounds

Prep Time: 25 Minutes
Start to Finish: 2 Hours
   10 Minutes
2 coffee cakes (8 wedges each)

COFFEE CAKE
3 1/2 to 4 cups Gold Medal bread
   flour or all-purpose flour
1/3 cup sugar
1 teaspoon salt

1 package regular active
   or fast-acting dry yeast
   (2 1/4 teaspoons)
1/3 cup vegetable shortening
1/2 cup water
1/2 cup milk
1 egg

CREAM CHEESE FILLING
1 package (8 oz) cream cheese
   or 1/3-less-fat cream cheese
   (Neufchâtel), softened

1/4 cup sugar
3 tablespoons Gold Medal
   all-purpose flour
1 egg yolk

TOPPING
1 can (21 oz) raspberry pie
   filling
1 egg white
1/2 cup sliced almonds
1/4 cup sugar

1 Grease bottoms and sides of 2 (9-inch) round cake pans with vegetable shortening or spray with cooking spray.

2 In large bowl, mix 2 cups of the flour, 1/3 cup sugar, the salt, and yeast; set aside.

3 In 1-quart saucepan, heat shortening, water, and milk over medium heat to 120°F to 130°F (shortening will not melt). Stir into flour mixture.

4 Add egg; beat with electric mixer on medium speed about 2 minutes or until smooth. Stir in enough of the remaining flour to make dough easy to handle. Turn dough onto lightly floured surface. Knead 3 to 5 minutes or until smooth. Cover and let rest 10 minutes.

5 In small bowl, mix all cream cheese filling ingredients; set aside.

6 Divide dough in half. Roll each half into 15-inch round. Fold each round into fourths; place each into one of the pans. Unfold; press dough against bottom and side of pan, allowing edge to hang over side. Spread half of the cream cheese filling over dough in each pan; top each with half of the pie filling.

{ recipe continues }

7 For each coffee cake, make cuts around edge of dough at 1-inch intervals to within ½ inch of filling. Twist strips of dough once or twice and fold over filling. Beat egg white until foamy; brush over dough. Sprinkle each coffee cake with ¼ cup almonds and 2 tablespoons sugar. Cover dough loosely with plastic wrap and let rise in warm place 45 minutes or until coffee cakes have doubled in size.

8 Heat oven to 375°F.

9 Bake 30 to 35 minutes or until golden brown. Cool 20 minutes. Cut each round into 8 wedges. Cover and refrigerate any leftover coffee cake.

Make-Ahead Directions: Coffee cakes can be covered and refrigerated up to 24 hours before rising in Step 7. Unwrap and continue as directed with rising in Step 7 (rise time may be slightly longer).

1 Wedge Calories 300; Total Fat 12g (Saturated Fat 4.5g, Trans Fat 0g); Cholesterol 40mg; Sodium 210mg; Total Carbohydrate 42g (Dietary Fiber 3g); Protein 6g **Carbohydrate Choices:** 3

Early food photography, where the Home Services staff would prepare the food and shoot it in the Kitchens.

This homey breakfast casserole takes only 15 minutes to throw together. Want to go full-on holiday? Use both red and green bell peppers in the bake as well as for the topping. Serve it with fresh fruit and juice for a simple brunch anytime.

Ham and Egg Brunch Bake

Prep Time: 15 Minutes
Start to Finish: 45 Minutes
6 servings

BRUNCH BAKE
2 eggs
2 cups Bisquick Original Pancake & Baking Mix

1½ cups chopped cooked smoked ham (about 8 oz)
¾ cup shredded cheddar cheese (3 oz)
1 small onion, chopped (about ½ cup)
⅓ cup chopped green bell pepper

⅓ cup milk
2 tablespoons vegetable oil

TOPPINGS
¾ cup shredded cheddar cheese (3 oz)
2 tablespoons chopped green bell pepper

1 Heat oven to 375°F. Grease 9-inch square pan with vegetable shortening or spray with cooking spray.

2 In medium bowl, beat eggs slightly. Stir in remaining brunch bake ingredients. Spread evenly in pan.

3 Bake 22 to 26 minutes or until top is light brown. Sprinkle with toppings. Bake 1 to 2 minutes longer or until cheese is melted. Let stand 2 minutes. Cut into 3 rows by 2 rows.

1 Serving Calories 400; Total Fat 21g (Saturated Fat 8g, Trans Fat 0g); Cholesterol 110mg; Sodium 1090mg; Total Carbohydrate 33g (Dietary Fiber 1g); Protein 19g **Carbohydrate Choices:** 2

Lost Recipe Re-created

The title alone piqued our interest . . . and then the ingredients sealed the deal—we had to re-create this for Joanne! Also known as Frog Eye Salad, heavenly concoctions such as this one always contained tiny pasta, such as acini di pepe or small rings, that looked like eyes . . . and so the name stuck. A custard-like mixture coats luscious tropical fruit and pasta for an outstanding salad perfect for any special occasion or potluck.

Creamy Tropical Fruit Salad

Prep Time: 30 Minutes
Start to Finish: 1 Hour
   30 Minutes
12 servings (about ½ cup each)

1 cup uncooked large ring
   or ditalini (short tube)
   pasta (4 oz)

1 can (20 oz) pineapple chunks
   in juice
1 tablespoon cornstarch
½ teaspoon salt
1 egg yolk
¾ cup coconut, toasted*

1½ cups halved red or green
   seedless grapes
½ cup halved maraschino
   cherries without stems
1 cup heavy whipping cream
2 tablespoons sugar

1 Cook pasta as directed on package; drain. Rinse with cold water; drain well.

2 Meanwhile, drain pineapple, reserving juice. Cover and refrigerate pineapple.

3 In 1-quart saucepan, mix pineapple juice, cornstarch, and salt until smooth. Cook over medium heat, stirring frequently, until mixture is thick and bubbly. Cook and stir 1 minute; remove from heat. In small bowl, beat egg yolk with fork. Slowly stir ¼ cup of the pineapple mixture into beaten egg yolk. Return mixture to saucepan; mix well. Cook and stir over medium heat 1 minute.

4 In a large bowl, place cooked pasta. Pour pineapple sauce over pasta; toss to coat. Cover and refrigerate at least 1 hour but no longer than 24 hours.

5 Measure out 2 tablespoons toasted coconut and set aside. If desired, set aside a few pineapple pieces and grape halves for garnish. Gently stir remaining pineapple, grapes, coconut, and cherries into pasta mixture with large spoon, breaking up clumped pasta.

6 In medium bowl, beat whipping cream and sugar with electric mixer on low speed until mixture begins to thicken. Beat on medium speed just until soft peaks form. Fold whipped cream into pasta mixture. Garnish with reserved pineapple, grapes, and coconut. Cover and refrigerate any leftovers up to 2 days.

1 Serving Calories 200; Total Fat 9g (Saturated Fat 6g, Trans Fat 0g); Cholesterol 35mg; Sodium 150mg; Total Carbohydrate 27g (Dietary Fiber 1g); Protein 2g **Carbohydrate Choices:** 2

* To toast coconut: Heat oven to 350°F. Spread coconut in ungreased shallow pan. Bake uncovered 5 to 7 minutes, stirring occasionally, until golden brown.

Easy Tropical Fruit Salad: Omit the whipping cream and sugar and substitute 2 cups frozen (thawed) whipped topping.

Kitchen Notes: There was a lot of discussion in the Kitchens over what the right ingredients for the "custard" should be and which fruits should come together to make the prettiest and most flavorful combination. The delicious results made us smile . . . and kept us going back to taste it again!

Lost Recipe Memory

"My parents got the recipe from one of their trips to Florida 20 or more years ago. My father loved it so much he started making it for special occasions like Easter and Thanksgiving. My dad was not a cook but this one thing he really enjoyed making and that made it extra special because he wanted to share it with all the family. I would love this recipe but unfortunately after he passed I was never able to find it at his house or anywhere else."

—Joanne D.

From *Betty Crocker's Buffets* cookbook (1984), this scrumptious coconut chicken is easy enough to add sparkle to any weekday meal, yet special enough to serve guests. If you're feeding a crowd, you can double all the ingredients.

Coconut Chicken with Chutney

Prep Time: 15 Minutes
Start to Finish: 1 Hour
4 servings

4 (4- to 6-oz) boneless skinless chicken breasts
½ teaspoon salt
⅛ teaspoon ground coriander
⅛ teaspoon ground cumin

1 clove garlic, finely chopped
1 jar (8.5 oz) mango chutney
1 cup coconut
¼ cup buttermilk or milk
2 tablespoons butter, melted

1 Heat oven to 425°F. Grease 2-quart square glass baking dish or 11×7-inch (2-quart) glass baking dish with vegetable shortening or spray with cooking spray.

2 Between pieces of plastic wrap or waxed paper, place each chicken breast smooth side down; gently pound with flat side of meat mallet or roll until about ¼ inch thick. Remove top piece of plastic wrap; set aside.

3 In small bowl, mix salt, coriander, cumin, and garlic. Sprinkle about ¼ teaspoon on each chicken piece. Measure ½ cup of the chutney; drain and chop. Spoon about 1 tablespoon of chopped chutney on center of each chicken piece. Fold long sides over chutney; fold ends up and secure with toothpicks. Place coconut in shallow dish. Dip each chicken roll in buttermilk; shake off excess. Roll in coconut to coat all sides. Place seam side down in pan. Drizzle butter over chicken.

4 Cover and bake 30 minutes. Uncover and bake about 20 minutes or until chicken is no longer pink in center. Serve with remaining chutney.

Betty's Cooking Tip: Chutney makes this coconut chicken extra-special. It's a condiment made with fruit, sugar, and spices. Look for jars of it near the other condiments in larger grocery stores or near the international ingredients.

Make-Ahead Directions: Prepare as directed, except do not drizzle with butter in Step 3. Cover and refrigerate no longer than 24 hours. Uncover, drizzle with butter. Continue as directed in Step 4.

1 Serving Calories 400; Total Fat 17g (Saturated Fat 12g, Trans Fat 0g); Cholesterol 85mg; Sodium 620mg; Total Carbohydrate 33g (Dietary Fiber 2g); Protein 27g **Carbohydrate Choices:** 2

Nothing says holiday like the perfectly cooked roast. We've got you covered with easy-to-follow directions, no matter how you like it done, and a delectable sauce that makes the roast sing with flavor.

Peppered Beef Roast with Horseradish Sauce

Prep Time: 10 Minutes
Start to Finish: 2 Hours 10 Minutes
12 servings (1 serving beef and about 1 tablespoon sauce each)

ROAST

2 tablespoons black peppercorns, cracked

1 boneless beef sirloin tip roast (3 lb)

HORSERADISH SAUCE

¾ cup heavy whipping cream

3 tablespoons prepared horseradish

½ teaspoon ground mustard

¼ teaspoon salt

1 Heat oven to 325°F. Grease shallow roasting pan or broiler pan with vegetable shortening or spray with cooking spray.

2 Place peppercorns on large plate. Roll beef in pepper; press pepper into roast with heels of hands. Place roast on rack in pan. Insert ovenproof meat thermometer so tip is in thickest part of roast.

3 For medium-rare, roast uncovered about 1¾ hours or until thermometer reads 135°F. Remove from oven and cover loosely with foil; let stand 15 to 20 minutes until thermometer reads 145°F. For medium, roast uncovered about 2 hours until thermometer reads 150°F.

Remove from oven and cover loosely with foil; let stand 15 to 20 minutes until thermometer reads 160°F.

4 Meanwhile, mix all ingredients for horseradish sauce. Cover and refrigerate until ready to serve.

5 Transfer roast from pan to cutting board; cut into slices. Serve with horseradish sauce.

Make-Ahead Directions: Prepare roast as in Step 2 except do not insert thermometer. Cover and refrigerate up to 24 hours. Unwrap and insert thermometer as directed in Step 2. Continue with Step 3.

1 Serving Calories 190; Total Fat 9g (Saturated Fat 4.5g, Trans Fat 0g); Cholesterol 85mg; Sodium 130mg; Total Carbohydrate 1g (Dietary Fiber 0g); Protein 27g **Carbohydrate Choices:** 0

Why change up what works well? This roast from our 1988 Christmas cookbook still makes an easy-yet-delicious star of your holiday table, with its simple, flavor-packed herb coating. So yum!

Savory Pork Roast

Prep Time: 10 Minutes
Start to Finish: 2 Hours
16 servings

1 boneless pork loin roast (4 lb)
1 clove garlic, cut in half
1 teaspoon dried sage leaves

1 teaspoon dried marjoram leaves
1 teaspoon salt

1 Heat oven to 350°F. Grease shallow roasting pan or broiler pan with vegetable shortening or spray with cooking spray. Rub roast with cut sides of garlic.

2 In small bowl, mix herbs and salt. Sprinkle on roast on all sides. Place roast on rack in pan. Insert ovenproof meat thermometer so tip is in thickest part of roast.

3 Roast uncovered until thermometer reads 145°F to 160°F, 1 hour 20 minutes to 1 hour 40 minutes. Transfer from rack to cutting board. Cover loosely with foil; let stand at least 3 minutes before slicing.

1 Serving Calories 180; Total Fat 9g (Saturated Fat 3g, Trans Fat 0g); Cholesterol 70mg; Sodium 190mg; Total Carbohydrate 0g (Dietary Fiber 0g); Protein 25g **Carbohydrate Choices:** 0

The Scandinavian Kitchen of the Betty Crocker Kitchens, 1966–1973.

These cute-as-a-button breads appeared in the 1988 *Betty Crocker Christmas Cookbook*. They are an adaptation of a New Year's bread that originated in St. Albans, England, known as "Pope Ladies." They are fun to make and so delicious to sink your teeth into.

Snowman Buns

Prep Time: 30 Minutes
Start to Finish: 1 Hour
  30 Minutes
12 buns

1 package regular active
  or fast-acting dry yeast
  (2¼ teaspoons)

¾ cup warm water
  (100°F to 110°F)
⅓ cup sugar
¼ cup vegetable shortening
3 eggs
2 teaspoons ground nutmeg,
  if desired

1 teaspoon salt
3½ cups Gold Medal
  all-purpose flour
60 dried currants

1 In large bowl, dissolve yeast in warm water; let stand 5 minutes. Add sugar, shortening, 2 of the eggs, the nutmeg, salt, and 2 cups of the flour. Beat with an electric mixer on low speed, scraping bowl constantly, 30 seconds. Beat on medium speed, scraping bowl occasionally, 2 minutes. Stir in remaining 1½ cups flour until smooth. Cover with plastic wrap and let rise in a warm place about 45 minutes or until doubled in size. Dough is ready if indentation remains when touched.

2 Beat dough with wooden spoon 25 strokes to deflate. Turn onto well-floured surface; cut into 12 equal parts. For each snowman, twist off half of 1 dough part; shape into 2-inch oval for body. Shape one half of the remaining dough into a ball for the head; press into body. Press in tiny piece of dough for the nose. Shape the remaining dough into 4-inch-long roll; cut in half for arms. Press each into side of snowman for arms. Repeat with remaining dough parts.

3 Grease cookie sheet with vegetable shortening or spray with cooking spray; arrange snowmen about 3 inches apart on cookie sheet. Cover loosely with plastic wrap and let rise in warm place about 45 minutes or until rolls have doubled in size.

4 Meanwhile, heat oven to 350°F.

5 For each snowman, gently press 2 currants into head for eyes and 3 currants into body for buttons. Beat remaining egg; brush top and sides of snowman with egg.

6 Bake about 15 minutes or until golden brown. Remove from cookie sheet to cooling rack. Serve warm or cool.

1 Bun Calories 220; Total Fat 6g (Saturated Fat 1.5g, Trans Fat 0g); Cholesterol 45mg; Sodium 210mg; Total Carbohydrate 35g (Dietary Fiber 1g); Protein 5g **Carbohydrate Choices:** 2

From *Betty Crocker Holidays* (1994) magazine. "This delicious bread is the perfect addition to a holiday brunch. Slice up one loaf, wrap the other to give away." The loaves make a yummy gift for teachers, the mail carrier, or neighbors.

Eggnog–Poppy Seed Bread

Prep Time: 10 Minutes
Start to Finish: 3 Hours 15 Minutes
2 small loaves (12 slices each) *or 1 large loaf* (16 slices)

2½ cups Gold Medal all-purpose flour
1¼ cups dairy eggnog
1 cup sugar
¼ cup poppy seed
3 tablespoons vegetable oil

1 tablespoon plus 1 teaspoon orange zest
3½ teaspoons baking powder
1 teaspoon salt
1 teaspoon ground nutmeg
1 egg

1 Heat oven to 350°F. Grease bottom only of two (8×4-inch) or one (9×5-inch) loaf pan with vegetable shortening or spray with cooking spray.

2 In large bowl, mix all ingredients with spoon; beat 30 seconds. Pour into pan(s).

3 Bake 8-inch loaves 55 to 60 minutes, 9-inch loaf 55 to 65 minutes or until toothpick inserted in center comes out clean. Cool 10 minutes in pan(s) on cooling rack.

4 Loosen sides of loaf from pan(s); remove pan(s) and place top side up on cooling rack. Cool completely, about 2 hours, before slicing. Wrap tightly and store in refrigerator up to 1 week.

Make-Ahead Directions: Wrap completely cooled, tightly wrapped bread in resealable freezer plastic bags up to 3 months. Thaw by loosening wrap and let stand at room temperature 2 to 3 hours.

1 Slice (from small loaf) Calories 130; Total Fat 3.5g (Saturated Fat 1g, Trans Fat 0g); Cholesterol 15mg; Sodium 190mg; Total Carbohydrate 21g (Dietary Fiber 0g); Protein 2g **Carbohydrate Choices:** 1½

We were so curious about what this bread would be like, we had to take on the challenge of re-creating it from Wendy S.'s memories of it. Such a jolly and decadent treat! Whether served as a holiday breakfast bread or for dessert, the jewel-tone colors of the gumdrops add merriment whenever you serve it.

Gumdrop Bread

Prep Time: 35 Minutes
Start to Finish: 3 Hours
  55 Minutes
2 loaves (12 slices each)

BREAD
2 cups assorted fruit-flavored
  gumdrops (from two 6.5-oz
  boxes)

3¼ cups Gold Medal
  all-purpose flour
1 teaspoon baking powder
½ teaspoon salt
2½ cups granulated sugar
1 cup butter, softened
1 teaspoon vanilla
5 eggs
1 cup milk

1 can (8 oz) crushed pineapple
  in juice, drained (⅔ cup)
1 cup coconut

GLAZE
1 cup powdered sugar
4 to 5 teaspoons milk

1 Heat oven to 325°F. Generously grease bottom and sides of 2 (9×5-inch) loaf pans with shortening or spray with cooking spray; lightly flour.

2 Using scissors, cut candies in half and place in medium bowl. Toss with ¼ cup of the flour to coat; set aside.

3 In another medium bowl, mix the remaining 3 cups flour, baking powder, and salt. In large bowl, beat granulated sugar, butter, vanilla, and eggs with electric mixer on low speed 30 seconds; scrape bowl. Beat on high speed 5 minutes, scraping bowl occasionally. Add flour mixture alternately with milk, beating on low speed just until smooth after each addition. Fold in candy mixture, pineapple, and coconut. Divide batter evenly between pans.

4 Bake 1 hour 10 minutes to 1 hour 15 minutes or until toothpick inserted in center comes out clean. Cool 20 minutes; loosen edges of cake from pans with metal spatula. Remove from pans to cooling rack. Cool completely, about 1½ hours.

5 In a small bowl, place powdered sugar. Stir in milk, 1 teaspoon at a time, until desired drizzling consistency. Drizzle over loaves. Cut loaves into slices using a serrated knife.

1 Slice Calories 330; Total Fat 10g (Saturated Fat 6g, Trans Fat 0g); Cholesterol 60mg; Sodium 160mg; Total Carbohydrate 55g (Dietary Fiber 0g); Protein 3g **Carbohydrate Choices:** 3½

Kitchen Notes: In our testing, we found that the boxed gumdrops were the perfect size and texture for this bread. For ease when serving and to keep the gumdrops from falling to the bottom of the loaves, we cut the gumdrops in half and tossed them with some of the flour before mixing them into the batter.

Lost Recipe Memory

"My mom made it every year at Christmas time."

—Wendy S.

These little spice gems taste "like biting into a little fruitcake," according to the 1988 *Betty Crocker Christmas* cookbook. We think these are so much more! A homey molasses and spice flavor in a soft, moist cookie with loads of candied fruit and nuts. It's a knock-out combination.

Christmas Jewels

Prep Time: 20 Minutes
Start to Finish: 1 Hour 30 Minutes
About 6 dozen cookies

½ cup molasses
⅓ cup vegetable shortening
¼ cup sugar

1 egg
1½ cups Gold Medal all-purpose flour
1 teaspoon ground cinnamon
1 teaspoon ground mace or nutmeg
1 teaspoon ground nutmeg
½ teaspoon baking soda

¼ teaspoon salt
¼ teaspoon ground allspice
¼ teaspoon ground ginger
2½ cups diced mixed candied fruit (about 16 oz)
2 cups coarsely chopped nuts

1 Heat oven to 325°F. Lightly grease 2 cookie sheets with vegetable shortening or spray with cooking spray.

2 In medium bowl, mix molasses, shortening, sugar, and egg. Stir in remaining ingredients except candied fruit and nuts. Stir in candied fruit and nuts. Onto each cookie sheet, drop dough by teaspoonfuls, about 1 inch apart.

3 Bake 1 cookie sheet 12 to 15 minutes or until set. Remove cookies from cookie sheet to cooling rack. Repeat with second cookie sheet.

4 Onto completely cooled cookie sheets, continue forming and baking cookies as directed in Steps 2 and 3.

How to Store: Store these cookies in a tightly covered container at room temperature.

1 Cookie Calories 70; Total Fat 3g (Saturated Fat 0g, Trans Fat 0g); Cholesterol 0mg; Sodium 25mg; Total Carbohydrate 10g (Dietary Fiber 0g); Protein 1g **Carbohydrate Choices:** ½

Why add liquor to cookies such as these? Liquor was added to vintage recipes such as fruit cake and cookies for both flavor and character. You'll be tempted to eat them right away . . . but hold back. The brandy mellows over time and marries beautifully with the other ingredients to create a delicious combination.

No-Bake Brandy-Walnut Balls

Prep Time: 20 Minutes
Start to Finish: 5 Days
  20 Minutes
About 5 dozen balls

3 cups finely crushed vanilla
  wafers (about 84 wafers)
2 cups powdered sugar
1 cup finely chopped walnuts
1/4 cup unsweetened baking
  cocoa

1/2 cup brandy
1/4 cup light corn syrup
Granulated, powdered,
  or colored sugar

1 In large bowl, mix wafers, powdered sugar, walnuts, and cocoa with spoon. Stir in brandy and corn syrup. In shallow bowl, place granulated sugar.

2 Shape level tablespoonfuls of wafer mixture into 1-inch balls; roll in sugar. Place in airtight container. Store at room temperature at least 5 days to blend flavors.

How to Store: Place in airtight container. Store at room temperature up to 4 weeks.

1 Ball Calories 60; Total Fat 2g (Saturated Fat 0g, Trans Fat 0g); Cholesterol 0mg; Sodium 15mg; Total Carbohydrate 8g (Dietary Fiber 0g); Protein 0g **Carbohydrate Choices:** 1/2

From our 1990 *Holiday Cookies* magazine, these delightful sweet-salty cookie bars might remind you of a certain salted peanut candy roll that's been around for nearly 100 years. The contrasting textures and flavors in this bar are sure to be a hit whenever you serve them.

Nutty Marshmallow Bars

Prep Time: 15 Minutes
Start to Finish: 2 Hours
   45 Minutes
24 bars

1 cup chopped salted cocktail
   peanuts
¾ cup Gold Medal
   all-purpose flour
¾ cup quick-cooking or
   old-fashioned oats
⅔ cup packed brown sugar

½ teaspoon baking soda
½ teaspoon salt
1 egg
⅓ cup butter, softened
1 jar (7 oz) marshmallow creme
⅔ cup caramel topping
1½ cups salted cocktail peanuts

1 Heat oven to 350°F.

2 In large bowl, mix 1 cup chopped peanuts, the flour, oats, brown sugar, baking soda, salt, and egg with spoon until blended. Cut in butter, using fork, until mixture is crumbly. In ungreased 13×9-inch pan, press mixture evenly on bottom of pan.

3 Bake 10 minutes.

4 Spoon marshmallow creme by spoonfuls over hot baked crust. Let stand 1 minute; spread evenly. Drizzle caramel topping over marshmallow creme. Sprinkle with 1½ cups peanuts.

5 Bake about 20 minutes or until golden brown.

6 Cool completely in pan on cooling rack, about 1½ hours. Loosen edges from sides of pan. Using wet knife, cut into 6 rows by 4 rows.

How to Store: Store covered at room temperature.

1 Bar Calories 220; Total Fat 11g (Saturated Fat 3g, Trans Fat 0g); Cholesterol 15mg; Sodium 200mg; Total Carbohydrate 26g (Dietary Fiber 1g); Protein 5g **Carbohydrate Choices:** 2

This adorable cookie recipe from a 1993 *Holiday Baking* magazine got lost before we created a recipe database of the thousands of recipes we've developed in the Betty Crocker Kitchens. We're so glad we found it—you'll love these treats as part of your holiday cookie platter.

Almond-Filled Crescents

Prep Time: 40 Minutes
Start to Finish: 3 Hours
  5 Minutes
4 dozen cookies

COOKIES
1 cup powdered sugar
1 cup heavy whipping cream
2 eggs
3¾ cups Gold Medal
  all-purpose flour
1 teaspoon baking powder
½ teaspoon salt

1 package (8 oz) almond paste
¾ cup butter, softened

GLAZE
1 cup powdered sugar
6 to 7 teaspoons milk
Sliced almonds, if desired

1 In large bowl, mix 1 cup powdered sugar, the whipping cream, and eggs until well blended. Stir in flour, baking powder, and salt (dough will be stiff). Divide dough into 4 equal parts; press each part into a round. Cover and refrigerate rounds about 1 hour or until firm.

2 Heat oven to 375°F.

3 In medium bowl, break almond paste into small pieces; add butter. Beat with electric mixer on low speed until blended. Beat on high speed until fluffy (tiny bits of almond paste will still be visible).

4 On lightly floured surface, roll one round of dough at a time into 10-inch round. Spread about ½ cup almond paste mixture on a dough round. Cut into 12 wedges. For each cookie, roll up wedge, beginning at wide edge. Onto ungreased cookie sheet, arrange cookies, point side down, about 2 inches apart. Curve cookies to form crescents.

5 Bake 14 to 16 minutes or until golden brown. Remove cookies from cookie sheet to cooling rack. Cool completely.

6 Onto completely cooled cookie sheet, prepare remaining dough rounds and almond paste mixture as directed in Step 4. Arrange on cooled cookie sheet and bake cookies as directed in Step 5.

7 In small bowl, mix 1 cup powdered sugar and 1 tablespoon of the milk until smooth. Stir in additional milk, 1 teaspoon at a time, until glaze is drizzling consistency. Drizzle over cookies. Immediately sprinkle with sliced almonds.

{ recipe continues }

How to Store: Before storing, let glaze set, about 2 hours. Place in airtight container, with waxed paper between layers.

1 Cookie Calories 120; Total Fat 6g (Saturated Fat 3g, Trans Fat 0g); Cholesterol 20mg; Sodium 40mg; Total Carbohydrate 15g (Dietary Fiber 0g); Protein 2g **Carbohydrate Choices:** 1

During the 1970s and 1980s, Betty Crocker published several books about flowers and gardening.

The predecessor to trifle, tipsy squire is also known as tipsy pudding, tipsy parson, or squire cake. The fluffy cake is split shortcake style, filled with liquor-laced custard sauce, and topped with whipped cream and almonds. Dreamy!

Tipsy Squire

Prep Time: 40 Minutes
Start to Finish: 2 Hours
   5 Minutes
9 servings

2½ cups milk
2 tablespoons sherry, Marsala wine, rum, Cognac, or whiskey

½ cup warm milk
½ teaspoon vanilla
¼ cup butter, melted

SHERRY CUSTARD SAUCE
2 whole eggs
2 egg yolks
⅓ cup sugar
Dash salt

CAKE
1½ cups Gold Medal all-purpose flour
1 teaspoon baking powder
3 eggs
1 cup sugar

TOPPINGS
½ cup heavy whipping cream
½ cup slivered almonds, toasted*
Fresh raspberries, if desired
Fresh mint leaves, if desired

1 In 2-quart saucepan, mix 2 whole eggs, the egg yolks, ⅓ cup sugar, and salt. Gradually stir in 2½ cups milk. Cook over medium-low heat, stirring constantly, just to boiling; remove from heat. Stir in sherry. Pour into heatproof glass bowl. Cover and refrigerate at least 2 hours but no longer than 24 hours.

2 Meanwhile, heat oven to 350°F. Line bottom of 9-inch square pan with cooking parchment paper.

3 In small bowl, mix flour and baking powder; set aside. In large bowl, beat 3 eggs and 1 cup sugar with electric mixer on high speed, scraping bowl occasionally, about 3 minutes or until thick and lemon colored. Beat in warm milk and vanilla on low speed. Beat in flour mixture; gently stir in melted butter. Pour into pan.

4 Bake about 25 minutes or until toothpick inserted in center comes out clean. Cool in pan 10 minutes. Remove from pan to cooling rack; cool completely, about 1 hour.

5 In small bowl, beat whipping cream with electric mixer on low speed until cream begins to thicken. Gradually increase speed to high and beat until stiff peaks form; set aside.

6 Cut cake into 3 rows by 3 rows. For each serving, with serrated knife, cut cake horizontally in half. Place bottom half on serving plate; top with 3 tablespoons of the custard sauce. Replace top of cake. Spoon remaining custard sauce over servings; top with whipped cream and almonds. Garnish with raspberries and mint leaves.

{ recipe continues }

* To toast almonds: Heat oven to 350°F. Spread nuts in ungreased shallow pan. Bake uncovered for 6 to 10 minutes, stirring occasionally, until light brown.

Make-Ahead Directions: Prepare as directed through Step 5. Cover cake. Cover and refrigerate whipped cream. Just before serving, continue with Step 6.

1 Serving Calories 410; Total Fat 18g (Saturated Fat 8g, Trans Fat 0g); Cholesterol 180mg; Sodium 210mg; Total Carbohydrate 52g (Dietary Fiber 1g); Protein 10g **Carbohydrate Choices:** 3½

From our *Holiday Baking* (1993) magazine, this indulgent cake is so named for a 19th-century Russian diplomat who had many indulgent recipes created for his lavish tastes, including a decadent pudding that contained candied fruit. Our holiday-worthy chocolate cake uses diced candied or dried fruits in a rich whipped cream filling with a fluffy cocoa frosting. It's festive and fabulous!

Chocolate Nesselrode Cake

Prep Time: 30 Minutes
Start to Finish: 2 Hours
   15 Minutes
16 servings

CAKE

2 cups Gold Medal
   all-purpose flour

2 cups sugar

½ cup vegetable shortening

1 teaspoon baking soda

1 teaspoon salt

½ teaspoon baking powder

¾ cup water

¾ cup buttermilk

1 teaspoon vanilla

2 eggs

4 oz unsweetened baking
   chocolate, melted, cooled

NESSELRODE FILLING

1 cup heavy whipping cream

¼ cup powdered sugar

1 teaspoon rum extract or
   1 tablespoon white or
   dark rum

¼ cup diced candied fruit
   and/or dried fruit (such as
   apricots or papaya)

COCOA FLUFF FROSTING

1 cup heavy whipping cream

¼ cup powdered sugar

2 tablespoons unsweetened
   baking cocoa

Additional diced candied or
   dried fruit, if desired

1 Heat oven to 350°F. Grease bottoms and sides of 3 (8-inch) round cake pans with vegetable shortening or spray with cooking spray; lightly flour.

2 In large bowl, beat all cake ingredients with electric mixer on low speed 30 seconds, scraping bowl constantly. Beat on high speed about 3 minutes, scraping bowl occasionally. Pour into pans.

3 Bake 30 to 35 minutes or until toothpick inserted in center comes out clean. Cool cake in pans 10 minutes. Remove from pans to cooling racks; cool completely, about 1 hour.

4 Meanwhile, in medium bowl, beat all filling ingredients except candied fruit with electric mixer on high speed until stiff. Fold in ¼ cup candied fruit.

5 In separate medium bowl, beat all frosting ingredients until stiff.

6 Place one cake layer, bottom side up, on plate. Spread one-third of filling to ¼ inch of edge. Repeat with second layer and one-third of filling. Place third layer rounded side up on cake; frost top with remaining filling.

7 Frost sides of cake with frosting. Sprinkle additional candied fruit on top of cake. Refrigerate cake uncovered until serving time. Cover and refrigerate any remaining cake.

9-inch Cake: Prepare as directed, except in Step 1, grease and flour 2 (9-inch) round cake pans. In Step 6, split cakes horizontally in half, using long serrated knife. Fill layers each with one-fourth of filling and frost top with remaining filling. Continue as directed in Step 7.

1 Serving Calories 400; Total Fat 21g (Saturated Fat 10g, Trans Fat 0g); Cholesterol 60mg; Sodium 280mg; Total Carbohydrate 47g (Dietary Fiber 2g); Protein 4g **Carbohydrate Choices:** 3

Refrigerator Ice Box Cake Print Advertisement, 1942.

MRS. PETER SIMONS, VIROQUA, WIS., SAYS:

"This is a gorgeous recipe! It's worth saving up sugar to make. Especially when you consider the very large number of servings the recipe makes. I used just half the recipe, which took only half a cup of sugar for the cake and half a cup for the rich filling. It's one of the best Betty Crocker recipes I ever tried. Gold Medal Flour gives it a lovely moist eating quality."

This light-as-a-cloud pie from *Betty Crocker's Holiday Baking* magazine (1993) has peppermint fluff filling in a chocolate crust. It's perfect for Valentine's Day or any Thanksgiving or Christmas gathering.

Pink Peppermint Pie

Prep Time: 30 Minutes
Start to Finish: 4 Hours
50 Minutes
8 servings

CHOCOLATE COOKIE CRUST
15 creme-filled chocolate
    sandwich cookies, finely
    crushed (1½ cups)
3 tablespoons butter, melted

PEPPERMINT FILLING
24 large marshmallows
½ cup milk

1 teaspoon vanilla
⅛ teaspoon salt
6 drops peppermint extract
6 drops red food color
1 cup heavy whipping cream
About 20 peppermint candies,
    coarsely crushed

1 In medium bowl, mix crushed cookies and melted butter. Press firmly against bottom and side of ungreased 9-inch glass pie plate.

2 In 2-quart saucepan, heat marshmallows and milk over low heat, stirring constantly, just until marshmallows are melted. Remove from heat; stir in vanilla, salt, peppermint extract, and food color. Refrigerate uncovered, stirring occasionally, about 20 minutes or until mixture mounds slightly when dropped from a spoon.

3 In medium bowl, beat whipping cream with electric mixer on low speed until cream begins to thicken. Gradually increase speed to high and beat until stiff peaks form. Fold marshmallow mixture into whipped cream. Spread filling in crust.

4 Refrigerate about 4 hours or until set. Just before serving, sprinkle with crushed candies. Cover and refrigerate any remaining pie.

1 Serving Calories 350; Total Fat 18g (Saturated Fat 10g, Trans Fat 0.5g); Cholesterol 50mg; Sodium 230mg; Total Carbohydrate 45g (Dietary Fiber 0g); Protein 2g **Carbohydrate Choices:** 3

Memorable Main Dishes

From *Betty Crocker's Complete Chicken Cookbook* (1994), we love this recipe when the summer air turns crisp. The homey goodness of all the savory flavors topped with cheddar dumplings is just too good to forget.

Chicken-Barley Stew with Cheddar Dumplings

Prep Time: 1 Hour
Start to Finish: 1 Hour
  10 Minutes
6 servings

STEW

1¼ lb boneless skinless chicken
  thighs (about 6)
1 can (14.5 oz) whole tomatoes,
  undrained
1 medium carrot, sliced (1 cup)
1 medium onion, chopped
  (1 cup)
½ cup quick-cooking barley

3½ cups chicken broth
1 tablespoon plus 1½ teaspoons
  chopped fresh or
  1½ teaspoons dried
  basil leaves
1 tablespoon chopped fresh or
  1 teaspoon dried sage leaves
¼ teaspoon black pepper
2 bay leaves
½ cup cold water
3 tablespoons Gold Medal
  all-purpose flour
2 medium zucchini, sliced
  (2 cups)

CHEDDAR DUMPLINGS

1½ cups Gold Medal
  all-purpose flour
2 teaspoons baking powder
½ teaspoon ground mustard
⅛ teaspoon salt
⅛ teaspoon ground red pepper
  (cayenne)
3 tablespoons cold butter or
  shortening
½ cup shredded sharp cheddar
  cheese
¾ cup milk

1 In 5- or 6-quart Dutch oven, mix all stew ingredients except cold water, 3 tablespoons flour, and zucchini; break up tomatoes. Heat to boiling; reduce heat. Cover and simmer, stirring occasionally, about 40 minutes or until juice of chicken is clear when thickest part is cut (at least 165°F). Discard bay leaves.

2 In small bowl, mix 1½ cups flour, baking powder, mustard, salt, and red pepper. Cut in butter, using pastry blender or fork, until mixture looks like fine crumbs. Stir in cheese. Stir in milk. Set aside.

3 In small bowl, stir cold water and 3 tablespoons flour until smooth. Gradually stir into chicken mixture. Heat to boiling, stirring constantly. Boil and stir 1 minute. Stir in zucchini. Heat to boiling. Drop dough by 6 spoonfuls onto hot chicken mixture. Cover and cook over low heat 10 minutes. Cover; cook 10 minutes longer or until dumplings are completely cooked in the center.

1 Serving Calories 460; Total Fat 15g (Saturated Fat 7g, Trans Fat 0g); Cholesterol 120mg; Sodium 1050mg; Total Carbohydrate 51g (Dietary Fiber 6g); Protein 30g **Carbohydrate Choices:** 3½

Your Share

How to prepare appetizing, healthful meals ★ ★ with foods available today ★ ★ ★

Betty Crocker

52 MENUS
226 RECIPES
369 HINTS

On Food Buying, Preparation, Meal Planning and Serving.

Seven million copies of Your Share cookbook were distributed during WWII, providing information to homemakers on how to use rations and making nutritious meals, regardless of what foods were available, and preventing food waste.

Bacon and noodles in a chicken stew? Yes, please! This is totally comfort food at its best.

Hearty Chicken Stew

Prep Time: 35 Minutes
Start to Finish: 1 Hour
15 Minutes
6 servings

3 slices bacon, cut into 1-inch
pieces
1 cut-up whole chicken
(3 to 3½ lb)

3 medium onions, thinly sliced
2 medium carrots, thinly sliced
(about 1 cup)
1 medium bell pepper (any
color), chopped (1 cup)
2 cups beer or nonalcoholic beer
2 cups chicken broth
1 tablespoon chopped fresh or
1 teaspoon dried thyme leaves

½ teaspoon pepper
6 oz uncooked dumpling egg
noodles (about 3 cups)
½ cup cold water
¼ cup Gold Medal
all-purpose flour
Additional fresh thyme leaves
and pepper, if desired

1 In 5- or 6-quart Dutch oven, cook bacon over medium heat, stirring frequently, until crisp. Remove bacon using a slotted spoon; drain on paper towels. (Do not drain bacon fat from Dutch oven.) Cook chicken in bacon drippings over medium heat about 15 minutes, turning occasionally, until browned on all sides. Remove from skillet; set aside. Cook onions in bacon fat over medium heat, stirring frequently, about 4 minutes or until crisp-tender. Stir in bacon, carrots, bell pepper, beer, broth, thyme, and pepper. Add chicken.

2 Heat to boiling; reduce heat. Cover and simmer 25 minutes. Heat to boiling; stir in noodles. Boil uncovered about 12 minutes or until juice of chicken is clear when thickest piece is cut to bone (at least 165°F) and noodles are tender.

3 In small bowl, stir water and flour until blended. Gradually stir into stew. Heat to boiling; boil and stir 1 minute. Sprinkle with additional fresh thyme leaves and pepper.

1 Serving Calories 420; Total Fat 17g (Saturated Fat 4.5g, Trans Fat 0g); Cholesterol 115mg; Sodium 480mg; Total Carbohydrate 32g (Dietary Fiber 3g); Protein 34g **Carbohydrate Choices:** 2

We love this twist on traditional lasagna with chicken, spinach, and a creamy white sauce from our 1994 *Great-Tasting Chicken* magazine. It's a cinch to put together and pop in the oven on a busy night.

Easy Chicken Lasagna

Prep Time: 15 Minutes
Start to Finish: 1 Hour
  35 Minutes
8 servings

1½ cups milk
1 can (10.5 oz) condensed cream
  of chicken soup
12 uncooked lasagna noodles
  (from 16-oz box)
⅔ cup grated Parmesan cheese

2 cups cut-up cooked chicken
  (about 10 oz)
⅛ teaspoon garlic powder
1 container (24 oz) reduced-fat
  cottage cheese
1 box (10 oz) frozen chopped
  spinach, thawed, squeezed
  to drain

1 Heat oven to 350°F.

2 In medium bowl, mix milk and soup until blended. Spread ½ cup of soup mixture in ungreased 13×9-inch (3-quart) glass baking dish. Top with 4 uncooked noodles.

3 Set aside ⅓ cup of Parmesan. In large bowl, mix remaining ingredients. Spread half of chicken mixture over noodles in dish; top with ½ cup soup mixture. Repeat with 4 uncooked noodles, remaining chicken mixture, and ½ cup soup mixture. Top with remaining uncooked noodles and soup mixture.

4 Cover with aluminum foil. Bake about 1 hour or until noodles are tender. Set oven control to broil. Sprinkle with reserved Parmesan. Place pan with top about 5 inches from heat. Broil 3 to 5 minutes or until top is beginning to brown. Uncover; let stand 15 minutes. Cut into 2 rows by 4 rows.

Make-Ahead Directions: Prepare as directed through Step 3. Cover with aluminum foil. Refrigerate up to 24 hours. To cook, continue as directed in Step 4, cooking until noodles are tender and center is hot. Broil as directed.

1 Serving Calories 360; Total Fat 11g (Saturated Fat 4.5g, Trans Fat 0g); Cholesterol 55mg; Sodium 710mg; Total Carbohydrate 36g (Dietary Fiber 2g); Protein 30g **Carbohydrate Choices:** 2½

Homemade pizza with scratch crust that's ready in 30 minutes? That's better than takeout. From our *Bisquick: Classics and New Favorites* magazine (1998), the barbecue chicken and veggie flavors of these individual pizzas are sure to be requested often in your home.

Individual Barbecue Chicken Pizzas

Prep Time: 10 Minutes
Start to Finish: 30 Minutes
4 servings (2 pizzas each)

CRUST

1½ cups Bisquick Original Pancake & Baking Mix

¼ cup grated Parmesan cheese

⅓ cup boiling water

1 tablespoon vegetable oil

TOPPINGS

1 cup shredded or diced cooked chicken (about 5 oz)

⅓ cup barbecue sauce

½ cup thinly sliced bell pepper (any color)

4 green onions, thinly sliced (¼ cup) or ¼ cup thinly sliced onion

¾ cup shredded Monterey Jack cheese (3 oz)

Sliced ripe olives, if desired

1 Heat oven to 375°F. Grease cookie sheet with vegetable shortening or spray with cooking spray.

2 In medium bowl, mix Bisquick mix and Parmesan. Stir in boiling water and oil until soft dough forms. Gather dough into a ball. Cut into fourths. Cut fourths in half; shape into balls. Onto cookie sheet, press each dough piece into 3-inch round about 2 inches apart.

3 In small bowl, mix chicken and barbecue sauce; spread over dough rounds to within ¼ inch of edges. Top with bell pepper, onions, Monterey Jack, and olives.

4 Bake 12 to 15 minutes or until crusts begin to brown.

1 Serving Calories 340; Total Fat 16g (Saturated Fat 7g, Trans Fat 0g); Cholesterol 55mg; Sodium 810mg; Total Carbohydrate 29g (Dietary Fiber 1g); Protein 19g **Carbohydrate Choices:** 2

Betty Crocker New England Kitchen
1966–1973.

Ohh . . . chicken parmigiana in a super-simple dinner pie. You'll love the easy preparation and comfort it brings! From our 1998 *Bisquick* magazine, the classic flavors of this dish are just as loved today.

Impossibly Easy Chicken Parmigiana Pie

Prep Time: 15 Minutes
Start to Finish: 55 Minutes
6 servings

1 cup chopped cooked chicken (about 5 oz)

1 cup shredded mozzarella cheese (4 oz)
1/4 teaspoon garlic powder
1/4 teaspoon dried basil leaves
1 cup tomato pasta sauce
2/3 cup Bisquick Original Pancake & Baking Mix

3/4 cup milk
1/2 cup small-curd cottage cheese
1/4 cup grated Parmesan cheese
2 eggs
1/4 teaspoon pepper

1 Heat oven to 400°F. Grease 9-inch pie plate with vegetable shortening or spray with cooking spray.

2 In medium bowl, mix chicken, 1/2 cup of the mozzarella cheese, the garlic powder, and basil; spread in bottom of pie plate. Pour pasta sauce over chicken mixture. In medium bowl, whisk together remaining ingredients except remaining 1/2 cup mozzarella cheese until blended. Pour over mixture in pie plate.

3 Bake 28 to 32 minutes or until knife inserted in center comes out clean. Top with remaining 1/2 cup mozzarella cheese. Bake 2 to 3 minutes longer or until cheese melts. Cool 5 minutes before serving.

1 Serving Calories 250; Total Fat 11g (Saturated Fat 5g, Trans Fat 0g); Cholesterol 105mg; Sodium 570mg; Total Carbohydrate 18g (Dietary Fiber 1g); Protein 19g **Carbohydrate Choices:** 1

From *Betty Crocker's Complete Chicken Cookbook* (1994). This clever recipe infuses chicken breast with flavor before using it in a dinner salad that is bursting with the goodness of fresh berries. Use the make-ahead directions below to get it on the table in no time.

Fresh Berry–Chicken Salad

Prep Time: 20 Minutes
Start to Finish: 1 Hour
   55 Minutes
4 servings

RASPBERRY VINAIGRETTE
1/2 cup raspberry vinegar

1/3 cup seedless red
   raspberry jam
1/4 cup olive or vegetable oil
1/4 teaspoon salt

SALAD
4 (6- to 8-oz) boneless skinless
   chicken breasts

2 1/2 cups chicken broth
2 tablespoons raspberry
   vinegar
2 bags (9 oz each) romaine
   lettuce hearts
1 cup fresh raspberries
1 cup fresh strawberries,
   cut in half

1 In small bowl, beat all vinaigrette ingredients with whisk until well blended. Cover and refrigerate while preparing salad.

2 In 12-inch skillet, place chicken, broth, and 2 tablespoons raspberry vinegar. Heat to boiling; reduce heat. Cover and simmer 15 to 20 minutes or until juice of chicken is clear when center of thickest part is cut (at least 165°F). Remove from heat. Uncover skillet; cool chicken in broth 15 minutes. Refrigerate chicken in broth about 45 minutes or until cool.

3 Remove chicken from broth; discard broth. Cut chicken diagonally into 1/4-inch slices. Divide romaine among 4 serving plates. Arrange chicken on romaine. Top with berries. Stir vinaigrette; drizzle over salads.

Make-Ahead Directions: Prepare the vinaigrette as directed in Step 1. Cover and refrigerate up to 24 hours. Prepare the chicken as directed through Step 2, covering and refrigerating the chicken up to 24 hours. When ready to serve, continue as directed in Step 3.

1 Serving Calories 470; Total Fat 20g (Saturated Fat 3.5g, Trans Fat 0g); Cholesterol 110mg; Sodium 840mg; Total Carbohydrate 30g (Dietary Fiber 5g); Protein 41g **Carbohydrate Choices:** 2

July 1998
#141

Betty Crocker®

PHOTO
OF EVERY
RECIPE

NEW
CHICKEN
COOKBOOK

SASSY CHICKEN
SALADS
p. 26
19
EASY IDEAS
FOR CHICKEN
BREASTS! p. 95

Grilled Caesar
Chicken & Veggies, p. 9

Over 500 Betty Crocker and related brands cooking magazines
were published between 1972 and 2014. Sphere—The Betty Crocker
Magazine, the first of several magazines, "was dedicated to the
young minded homemaker of the day, whose interest and influence,
while centered in the home, go far beyond its boundaries."

The flavors from your favorite Chinese restaurant were used to make this craveable chicken recipe. We brought the recipe back again, in case you missed it, as it's that good!

Chinese-Inspired Barbecued Chicken

Prep Time: 10 Minutes
Start to Finish: 1 Hour
   10 Minutes
6 servings

3 tablespoons hoisin sauce
2 tablespoons apricot preserves
1 tablespoon honey
1½ teaspoons peanut or
   vegetable oil
1½ teaspoons oyster sauce
1½ teaspoons soy sauce

1½ teaspoons dry sherry
1½ teaspoons chile puree
   with garlic
1 teaspoon five-spice powder
1 clove garlic, finely chopped
1 cut-up whole chicken
   (3 to 3½ lb)

1 Heat oven to 325°F. Line broiler pan with aluminum foil. Spray rack of broiler pan with cooking spray.

2 In 1-quart saucepan, mix all ingredients except chicken. Heat over medium-low heat, stirring occasionally, until preserves are melted. Place chicken, skin side up, on rack in broiler pan. Brush with preserves mixture.

3 Bake uncovered, brushing occasionally with preserves mixture, about 1 hour or until juice of chicken is clear when thickest piece is cut to bone (at least 165°F). Discard any remaining preserves mixture.

Grilled Chinese Barbecued Chicken: Heat gas or charcoal grill to medium for indirect heat. Carefully brush grill rack with vegetable oil. Place chicken skin side up on grill. Brush with preserves mixture. Cover and grill 15 minutes; turn chicken. Brush with preserves mixture. Cover and grill 20 to 30 minutes longer or until juice of chicken is clear when thickest pieces are cut to bone (at least 165°F). Discard any remaining preserves mixture.

1 Serving Calories 280; Total Fat 15g (Saturated Fat 4g, Trans Fat 0g); Cholesterol 85mg; Sodium 300mg; Total Carbohydrate 9g (Dietary Fiber 0g); Protein 27g **Carbohydrate Choices:** ½

This recipe first appeared in our 1969 version of *Betty Crocker's Picture Cook Book*. Over the years, more variations have been added. For those of you who grew up eating this salad on summer evenings or at picnics or potlucks, we had to bring it back. If you haven't had it before, once you eat it, you'll be hooked, too!

Chicken Macaroni Salad

Prep Time: 20 Minutes
Start to Finish: 2 Hours 20 Minutes
6 servings

1½ cups uncooked elbow macaroni (6 oz)
1 package (10 oz) frozen green peas

1½ cups shredded cheddar cheese (6 oz)
1 cup cut-up cooked chicken or turkey (about 5 oz)
8 medium green onions, sliced (½ cup)
1 medium stalk celery, sliced (½ cup)
¾ cup mayonnaise or salad dressing

⅓ cup sweet pickle relish
½ teaspoon salt
3 cups finely shredded lettuce
4 slices bacon, crisply cooked and crumbled (⅓ cup)

1 Cook macaroni as directed on package, adding peas during last 3 minutes of cooking time. Drain; rinse with cold water to cool.

2 In large bowl, mix macaroni with remaining ingredients except lettuce and bacon. Cover and refrigerate at least 2 hours to blend flavors.

3 Just before serving, toss macaroni mixture with the lettuce and bacon.

Curried Chicken Macaroni Salad: Add 2 teaspoons curry powder with the salt.

Chicken-Pineapple Macaroni Salad: Substitute 2 cups fresh or canned (drained) bite-size pieces of pineapple for 2 cups of the lettuce. Omit bacon. If desired, serve salad over a quartered fresh pineapple piece. Sprinkle with chopped red bell pepper.

1 Serving Calories 570; Total Fat 35g (Saturated Fat 10g, Trans Fat 0g); Cholesterol 65mg; Sodium 820mg; Total Carbohydrate 42g (Dietary Fiber 4g); Protein 23g **Carbohydrate Choices:** 3

A lot of love must have gone into the development of this dish. It's the epitome of comfort in a casserole, with the taste of the fall and the holidays. Whether you make it for a family supper or for a small holiday gathering, let the soothing flavors slow you down enough to savor the meal and conversation.

Chicken with Wild Rice and Cranberry Stuffing

Prep Time: 15 Minutes
Start to Finish: 2 Hours 45 Minutes
6 servings (1 piece chicken and ½ cup stuffing each)

CHICKEN

2 tablespoons vegetable oil

1 tablespoon chopped fresh or 1 teaspoon dried thyme leaves

1 tablespoon chopped fresh or 1 teaspoon dried marjoram leaves

¼ teaspoon salt

⅛ teaspoon pepper

1 whole chicken (4 to 5 lb)

STUFFING

¾ cup uncooked wild rice

1¾ cups chicken broth

½ cup coarsely chopped fresh cranberries

2 medium stalks celery, thinly sliced (1 cup)

1 small onion, chopped (½ cup)

2 tablespoons packed brown sugar

1 teaspoon orange zest

¼ cup orange juice

½ teaspoon ground nutmeg

⅓ cup coarsely chopped pecans or slivered almonds, toasted*

1 Heat oven to 375°F. Grease 1½-quart casserole with butter or spray with cooking spray.

2 In small bowl, mix oil, thyme, marjoram, salt, and pepper. Fold wings across back of chicken so tips are touching. Skewer or tie legs together. Place chicken, breast side up, on rack in shallow roasting pan or 13×9-inch pan fitted with rack. Brush herbed oil mixture on chicken. Insert ovenproof meat thermometer so tip is in thickest part of thigh and does not touch bone; set aside.

3 In 1½-quart saucepan, heat wild rice and broth over high heat to boiling, stirring once or twice; reduce heat. Cover and simmer 30 minutes, stirring occasionally. Stir in remaining stuffing ingredients except pecans. Cover and simmer 10 to 20 minutes, stirring occasionally, until liquid is absorbed and vegetables are just tender. Stir in pecans. Spoon into casserole.

4 Meanwhile, roast chicken uncovered 1 hour 15 minutes to 1 hour 30 minutes or until thermometer reads at least 165°F or legs move easily when lifted or twisted. Bake stuffing uncovered in oven with chicken during last 10 minutes of roasting time.

5 Cover chicken loosely with foil; let stand 15 to 20 minutes. (Continue to bake stuffing while chicken rests.) Serve chicken with stuffing.

* To toast nuts: Heat oven to 350°F. Spread nuts in ungreased shallow pan. Bake uncovered 6 to 10 minutes, stirring occasionally, until light brown.

Betty's Cooking Tip: Wild rice is actually not a rice, but an aquatic grass native to North America that has a nutty, earthy flavor and chewy texture. It is more expensive than regular rice because of its more limited supply.

1 Serving Calories 680; Total Fat 37g (Saturated Fat 9g, Trans Fat 1g); Cholesterol 180mg; Sodium 550mg; Total Carbohydrate 27g (Dietary Fiber 3g); Protein 60g **Carbohydrate Choices:** 2

Molly T.'s description of this fried chicken sounded so delicious and unique, we had to develop it for her! We worked and worked to get the right texture and flavor she described. The resulting hush puppy–like battered chicken was really something special. Originally, this was served in the restaurant as a half chicken, but we made it with drumsticks and breasts for home cooks. We hope we did Grandma Hershey proud, Molly!

Hush Puppy–Fried Chicken

Prep Time: 1 Hour
Start to Finish: 1 Hour
6 servings

CHICKEN

1¼ lb chicken drumsticks
2 boneless skinless chicken
   breasts (about 1 lb), cut in half
   crosswise
¼ teaspoon salt
¼ teaspoon black pepper
¾ cup Gold Medal
   all-purpose flour

DRY INGREDIENTS FOR COATING

1¼ cups Gold Medal
   all-purpose flour
1 cup cornmeal
2 tablespoons sugar
2½ teaspoons Old Bay
   seasoning
1 teaspoon garlic powder
½ teaspoon baking powder
½ teaspoon salt
½ teaspoon onion powder

¼ teaspoon ground red pepper
   (cayenne)

WET INGREDIENTS FOR COATING

1¾ cups plus
   2 tablespoons milk
2 tablespoons butter, melted
1 egg
2 tablespoons finely chopped
   parsley
Additional finely chopped
   parsley, if desired

1 Pat chicken dry with paper towels; sprinkle with salt and black pepper. In large food-safe plastic bag, place ¾ cup flour; set aside. In large bowl, mix dry ingredients for coating with whisk until blended.

2 In medium bowl, beat 1¾ cups of the milk, the melted butter, and egg with whisk until well blended. Stir in 2 tablespoons parsley. Add wet ingredients to dry ingredients; stir with whisk until blended and smooth.

3 In 5½- to 6-quart Dutch oven, heat 3 to 4 inches oil to 325°F. Place chicken drumsticks in bag with the flour; shake to coat chicken. Shake excess flour off one piece of chicken and dip it into the batter to coat, letting excess drip into the bowl. Carefully place in hot oil. Repeat with remaining drumsticks. Fry chicken 5 minutes, turning once. Remove from oil; drain on paper towels. Stir the 2 tablespoons milk into batter. Repeat coating and frying chicken breast pieces.

{ recipe continues }

4 If batter has thickened, stir in an additional tablespoon of milk. Dip fried chicken drumsticks again in batter to coat, letting excess drip into the bowl; carefully place back in hot oil. Fry 7 to 8 minutes, turning once, until thickest portion is at least 165°F. Drain on paper towels. Repeat with the fried chicken breast pieces. Fry 5 to 6 minutes, turning once, until thickest portion is at least 165°F. Sprinkle with additional finely chopped parsley.

Kitchen Notes: To get the ultimate coating and texture, we battered and fried the chicken twice. This also helps to cook large pieces of chicken all the way through without the coating becoming overdone. The batter will thicken over time, so be sure to thin it as directed in the recipe.

1 Serving Calories 640; Total Fat 26g (Saturated Fat 8g, Trans Fat 0g); Cholesterol 160mg; Sodium 740mg; Total Carbohydrate 61g (Dietary Fiber 2g); Protein 40g **Carbohydrate Choices:** 4

Lost Recipe Memory

"Hershey's was a small restaurant in Gaithersburg, Maryland, in the '80s by the Washington Grove railroad crossing bridge. Grandma Hershey . . . gave her recipe to our mom. Mom made it her own for 25 years but passed without writing it down or telling us! It's just the best Maryland Fried Chicken ever!"

—Molly T.

Our Consumer Care team had requests to bring back this homestyle dinner, all done in one pan. Originally appearing in the 1956 version of *Betty Crocker's Picture Cook Book*, the welcoming flavors of oven-fried chicken, biscuits, and spiced peaches is like a warm hug from Grandma! We love how easy it is to throw together. All you need is a salad or vegetable and dinner is done.

Oven-Baked Chicken and Biscuits

Prep Time: 15 Minutes
Start to Finish: 1 Hour
5 Minutes
6 servings (1 piece chicken and 1 biscuit each)

CHICKEN
½ cup butter
1 cup Gold Medal all-purpose flour
2 teaspoons paprika
1½ teaspoons salt
¼ teaspoon pepper
1 cut-up whole chicken (3 to 3½ lb)

1 can (15.25 oz) peach halves in heavy syrup, drained
6 whole cloves

BISCUITS
2 cups Bisquick Original Pancake and Baking Mix
⅔ cup milk
1 tablespoon vegetable oil

1 Heat oven to 425°F. In 13×9-inch pan, melt butter in oven.

2 In shallow dish, mix flour, paprika, salt, and pepper. Coat chicken with flour mixture. Place chicken, skin side down, in pan.

3 Bake uncovered 35 minutes.

4 Meanwhile, in medium bowl, mix Bisquick mix, milk, and oil.

5 Turn chicken skin side up and push to one end of pan. Top with peach halves, cut side up. Place a whole clove in middle of each peach half. Drop dough by large spoonfuls onto open side of pan.

Fan Memory
"When my kids were little (in the 1970s and '80s), they LOVED this recipe and we made it often."
—Cindy D.

{ recipe continues }

6 Bake 12 to 15 minutes or until juice of chicken is clear when thickest piece is cut to bone (at least 165°F) and biscuits are golden brown.

1 Serving Calories 660; Total Fat 31g (Saturated Fat 14g, Trans Fat 1g); Cholesterol 130mg; Sodium 1240mg; Total Carbohydrate 60g (Dietary Fiber 2g); Protein 34g **Carbohydrate Choices:** 4

Betty Crocker Kitchens staff answering consumer letters, circa 1934.

If you love sweet and sour chicken, you'll love this grilled lemon version. From *Betty Crocker's Complete Chicken Cookbook*, this tangy recipe simply tastes like summer! Pair it with corn on the cob and watermelon slices for an easy meal.

Lemonade Ginger Chicken

Prep Time: 20 Minutes
Start to Finish: 1 Hour 45 Minutes
6 servings

½ can (12-oz size) frozen lemonade concentrate, thawed
¾ cup water
2 tablespoons finely chopped gingerroot
2 tablespoons vegetable oil
1½ teaspoons fennel seed

½ teaspoon salt
¼ teaspoon pepper
2 cloves garlic, finely chopped
1 tablespoon cornstarch
1 tablespoon water
6 (6- to 8-oz) boneless skinless chicken breasts

1 In 1-quart saucepan, mix all ingredients except cornstarch, 1 tablespoon water, and the chicken. Heat to boiling; reduce heat. Simmer uncovered 5 minutes, stirring frequently. In small bowl, mix cornstarch and 1 tablespoon water; stir into lemonade mixture. Heat to boiling; reduce heat. Simmer uncovered about 1 minute, stirring frequently, until sauce is slightly thickened; remove from heat. Cool 15 minutes.

2 Place chicken in shallow glass or plastic dish or heavy-duty resealable heatproof plastic bag. Pour lemonade mixture over chicken; turn chicken to coat with marinade. Cover dish or seal bag and refrigerate, turning chicken occasionally, at least 30 minutes but no longer than 24 hours.

3 Brush grill rack with vegetable oil. Heat gas or charcoal grill to medium for indirect heat.

4 Remove chicken from marinade; set marinade aside. Place chicken on grill and brush with marinade. Discard any remaining marinade. Close grill; cook, turning occasionally, 35 to 45 minutes or until juice of chicken is clear when thickest pieces are cut to bone (at least 165°F).

Betty's Cooking Tip: For extra-moist grilled chicken, use a pair of tongs instead of a fork to turn the pieces. A fork will pierce the meat and release the juices.

1 Serving Calories 310; Total Fat 10g (Saturated Fat 2.5g, Trans Fat 0g); Cholesterol 105mg; Sodium 300mg; Total Carbohydrate 16g (Dietary Fiber 0g); Protein 38g **Carbohydrate Choices:** 1

This clever recipe appeared on the backs of our sacks of flour. It's a batter that becomes a pizza crust—how easy is that? We're not sure how this one ever got lost, but we were very happy to bring it back!

Crazy Crust Pizza

Prep Time: 20 Minutes
Start to Finish: 50 Minutes
4 servings (2 slices each)

1 lb ground beef
    (at least 80% lean)
1½ cups sliced fresh
    mushrooms (about 4 oz)
¼ cup chopped onion
1 cup pizza sauce
1 cup Gold Medal
    all-purpose flour

¾ teaspoon Italian seasoning
¼ teaspoon salt
⅛ teaspoon pepper
⅔ cup milk
2 eggs
1½ cups shredded mozzarella
    cheese (6 oz)

1 Move oven rack to lowest position; heat oven to 425°F. Grease 12-inch pizza pan with vegetable shortening or spray with cooking spray; lightly flour.

2 In 12-inch skillet, cook beef, mushrooms, and onion over medium heat 8 to 10 minutes, stirring occasionally, until beef is thoroughly cooked. Drain; stir in pizza sauce. Set aside.

3 In small bowl, mix flour, ½ teaspoon of the Italian seasoning, the salt, pepper, milk, and

eggs; stir with spoon until blended. Pour batter into pan, tilting pan so batter covers bottom. Spoon beef mixture over batter.

4 Place pan on lowest rack; bake 18 to 23 minutes or until edges of crust are golden brown.

5 Sprinkle with cheese and remaining ¼ teaspoon Italian seasoning. Bake an additional 2 to 3 minutes or until cheese is melted. Cut into 8 slices.

1 Serving Calories 530; Total Fat 26g (Saturated Fat 11g, Trans Fat 1g); Cholesterol 190mg; Sodium 750mg; Total Carbohydrate 36g (Dietary Fiber 2g); Protein 40g **Carbohydrate Choices:** 2½

We're bringing back this favorite recipe from *Betty Crocker's Great Tasting Beef* magazine (1991). It's an easy recipe that's a yummy tummy filler for hungry family and friends. And who won't love the cheeseburger toppings?

Cheeseburger Deep-Dish Pizza

Prep Time: 20 Minutes
Start to Finish: 45 Minutes
4 servings (2 pieces each)

PIZZA DOUGH

1 package regular active dry yeast (2¼ teaspoons)

1 cup warm water (100°F to 110°F)

2½ cups Gold Medal all-purpose or whole wheat flour

2 tablespoons vegetable oil

1 teaspoon sugar

¾ teaspoon salt

PIZZA TOPPINGS

1 lb ground beef (at least 80% lean)

1 can (14.5 oz) diced tomatoes, drained

¼ cup chopped onion

1 tablespoon fresh or 1 teaspoon dried oregano leaves

½ teaspoon salt

¼ teaspoon pepper

⅛ teaspoon garlic powder

1½ cups shredded cheddar cheese (6 oz)

1 Heat oven to 425°F. Grease bottom and sides of 13×9-inch pan with vegetable shortening or spray with cooking spray.

2 In medium bowl, dissolve yeast in warm water. Stir in remaining pizza dough ingredients; beat vigorously with wooden spoon 20 strokes. Let stand while preparing toppings.

3 In 10-inch skillet, cook beef over medium-high heat, 5 to 7 minutes, stirring occasionally, until no longer pink. Drain; set aside. In medium bowl, mix remaining ingredients except cheese.

4 Press dough evenly on bottom and halfway up sides of pan. Sprinkle beef over dough. Spoon tomato mixture over beef; top with cheese.

5 Bake uncovered 20 to 25 minutes or until cheese is lightly browned. Cut into 2 rows by 4 rows.

Betty's Cooking Tip: Go for the whole burger experience! Top slices of this pizza with your favorite hamburger pickle slices, ketchup, and mustard, for the full cheeseburger adventure.

1 Serving Calories 740; Total Fat 35g (Saturated Fat 14g, Trans Fat 1g); Cholesterol 110mg; Sodium 1170mg; Total Carbohydrate 67g (Dietary Fiber 3g); Protein 39g **Carbohydrate Choices:** 4½

Hailing from our *Mexican Fast & Flavorful* 1994 magazine, you'll love these oven-baked chimichangas. They are as delicious as the traditional ones, but way easier to make and without all the added fat and calories of frying.

Baked Chimichangas

Prep Time: 40 Minutes
Start to Finish: 50 Minutes
6 chimichangas

FILLING
1 lb ground beef
   (at least 80% lean)
¼ cup finely chopped onion

1 tablespoon red wine vinegar
1 teaspoon ground red pepper
   (cayenne)
¼ teaspoon ground cinnamon
⅛ teaspoon ground cloves
1 can (4 oz) chopped green chiles
1 medium tomato, chopped
   (about ¾ cup)

TORTILLAS AND TOPPINGS
6 flour tortillas (9 or 10 inch),
   warmed
1 egg, beaten
2 tablespoons butter, softened
Pico de gallo or salsa, if desired
Shredded lettuce, if desired

1 In 10-inch skillet, cook ground beef and onion over medium heat 8 to 10 minutes, stirring occasionally, until beef is thoroughly cooked; drain. Stir in remaining filling ingredients. Heat to boiling; reduce heat. Simmer uncovered 20 minutes, stirring occasionally.

2 Heat oven to 500°F.

3 Spoon about ½ cup beef mixture onto center of each tortilla. Fold bottom end of tortilla up about 1 inch over beef mixture; fold right and left sides over folded end, overlapping. Fold remaining end down; brush edges with egg to seal. Brush each chimichanga with butter. In ungreased 15×10×1-inch pan, place chimichangas seam side down.

4 Bake uncovered 8 to 10 minutes or until tortillas begin to brown and filling is hot. Top with pico de gallo and lettuce.

1 Chimichanga Calories 380; Total Fat 18g (Saturated Fat 8g, Trans Fat 0.5g); Cholesterol 85mg; Sodium 600mg; Total Carbohydrate 34g (Dietary Fiber 2g); Protein 19g **Carbohydrate Choices:** 2

Sauerbraten, or "sour roast," is a German specialty made by marinating a roast in a sweet-and-sour sauce for 2 to 3 days before cooking. Our riff on this, from *Betty Crocker's Pasta Cookbook* (1995), takes the flavors of sauerbraten but makes it into a quick meatball and noodle dish that's perfect for a weeknight meal or an easy way to impress your guests.

Sauerbraten Meatballs and Noodles

Prep Time: 15 Minutes
Start to Finish: 40 Minutes
6 servings

1 lb ground beef or pork
   (at least 80% lean)
⅓ cup crushed gingersnaps
   (about 6 gingersnaps from
   16-oz pkg)

1 small onion, finely chopped
   (½ cup)
¼ cup water
½ teaspoon salt
¼ teaspoon pepper
6 oz uncooked egg noodles or
   spaetzle (about 3 cups)
1 cup beef broth

¼ cup apple cider vinegar
¼ cup crushed gingersnaps
   (about 4 gingersnaps)
1 tablespoon sugar
2 tablespoons raisins
Chopped fresh parsley,
   if desired

1 Heat oven to 400°F. Line broiler pan with aluminum foil. Spray rack of broiler pan with cooking spray.

2 In medium bowl, mix ground beef, ⅓ cup gingersnaps, the onion, water, salt, and pepper. Shape mixture into 24 meatballs. Place meatballs on rack.

3 Bake uncovered 20 to 25 minutes or until thoroughly cooked and no longer pink in center and instant-read meat thermometer inserted in center reads 160°F.

4 Meanwhile, cook and drain noodles as directed on package.

5 In 1½-quart saucepan, mix remaining ingredients except raisins and parsley. Cook over medium heat, stirring constantly, until mixture thickens and boils. Stir in raisins and meatballs. Heat until hot. Spoon over noodles; sprinkle with parsley.

1 Serving Calories 310; Total Fat 11g (Saturated Fat 4g, Trans Fat 0g); Cholesterol 65mg; Sodium 460mg; Total Carbohydrate 34g (Dietary Fiber 1g); Protein 18g **Carbohydrate Choices:** 2

"What makes Joe grow?" "Many things, including sunlight, rest, love—and food. Especially food that contains proteins, those "building blocks" our bodies need for growth and repair. . . . General Mills brings you Betty Crocker's advice on nutrition in the interest of your family's health and welfare. This is one phase of General Mills' nutrition service to teachers, students, parents, and the public." General Mills print ad, undated.

Our Consumer Care team received requests for this recipe from the 1969 *Betty Crocker Cookbook*. What makes it so memorable? It's the easy, well-seasoned beef sauce that simmers on the stove to create a worth-the-effort spaghetti families love.

Italian-Style Spaghetti

Prep Time: 20 Minutes
Start to Finish: 1 Hour
  20 Minutes
6 servings

1 lb ground beef
  (at least 80% lean)
1 medium onion, chopped
  (1 cup)

1 clove garlic, finely chopped
1 cup water
1 teaspoon sugar
¾ teaspoon salt
1 teaspoon dried oregano leaves
¾ teaspoon dried basil leaves
½ teaspoon dried marjoram
  leaves, if desired

¼ teaspoon dried rosemary
  leaves, if desired
1 bay leaf
1 can (8 oz) tomato sauce
1 can (6 oz) tomato paste
1 package (16 oz) spaghetti
Grated Parmesan cheese,
  if desired

1 In 10-inch skillet, cook beef, onion, and garlic over medium-high heat, stirring occasionally, for 5 to 7 minutes or until no longer pink; drain. Return to skillet; stir in remaining ingredients except spaghetti and cheese. Heat to boiling; reduce heat. Cover and simmer, stirring occasionally, 1 hour.

2 Meanwhile, cook and drain spaghetti as directed on package.

3 Serve sauce over spaghetti. Sprinkle with cheese.

Chicken Spaghetti: Omit ground beef. Heat 1 tablespoon vegetable oil in skillet over medium heat. Cook and stir onion and garlic 3 to 4 minutes, stirring frequently, or until softened. Stir in remaining ingredients except spaghetti and cheese. Heat to boiling; reduce heat. Cover and simmer 30 minutes. Stir in 1½ cups cut-up cooked chicken breast. Heat to boiling; reduce heat. Cover and simmer 30 minutes. Continue as directed in Step 2.

Make-Ahead Directions: After Step 1, cool sauce. Place sauce in food storage containers. Cover and refrigerate up to 2 days or freeze up to 4 months. Thaw frozen sauce in refrigerator overnight or in microwavable container on Low (30%), stirring occasionally. Place sauce in saucepan. Heat to boiling; reduce heat. Simmer uncovered 10 minutes. Continue as directed in Step 2.

1 Serving Calories 510; Total Fat 11g (Saturated Fat 3.5g, Trans Fat 0g); Cholesterol 45mg; Sodium 530mg; Total Carbohydrate 76g (Dietary Fiber 6g); Protein 27g **Carbohydrate Choices:** 5

This frequently requested recipe first appeared in the 1969 *Betty Crocker Cookbook,* where it was originally published as Waikiki Meatballs. This is a Hawaiian-inspired dish, named after the colorful neighborhood in Honolulu, Hawaii. This very flavorful and easy skillet meal impressed us when we tasted it during our testing—it's clear to see why it's been so requested!

Sweet-and-Sour Meatballs

Prep Time: 35 Minutes
Start to Finish: 50 Minutes
6 servings (3 meatballs)

MEATBALLS
1 lb ground beef
   (at least 80% lean)
½ cup unseasoned dry
   bread crumbs
½ cup milk
2 tablespoons finely chopped
   onion
¾ teaspoon salt
1 egg

SWEET-AND-SOUR SAUCE
½ cup packed brown sugar
1 tablespoon cornstarch
1 can (20 oz) pineapple chunks
   in pineapple juice, undrained
⅓ cup white vinegar
1 tablespoon soy sauce
1 medium green bell pepper,
   coarsely chopped

SERVE WITH
White or jasmine rice or
   cooked egg noodles,
   if desired

1 Heat oven to 400°F.

2 In medium bowl, mix all meatball ingredients. Shape mixture into 18 (1¾-inch) balls. In ungreased 13×9-inch pan, place meatballs.

3 Bake uncovered 20 to 25 minutes or until meatballs are thoroughly cooked and no longer pink in center. Drain if necessary; cover to keep warm.

4 Meanwhile, in 12-inch skillet, mix brown sugar and cornstarch. Stir in pineapple with juice, vinegar, and soy sauce. Heat to boiling, stirring constantly.

5 Add meatballs and bell pepper; reduce heat. Simmer uncovered, stirring occasionally, 13 to 15 minutes or until bell pepper is crisp-tender. Serve with cooked rice.

Betty's Cooking Tip: If you make smaller meatballs (and reduce the bake time), you can also use this as a wonderful appetizer with frilly toothpicks for picking up the meatballs— no rice needed!

1 Serving Calories 330; Total Fat 10g (Saturated Fat 4g, Trans Fat 0g); Cholesterol 80mg; Sodium 570mg; Total Carbohydrate 43g (Dietary Fiber 1g); Protein 17g **Carbohydrate Choices:** 3

Meat loaf is a classic recipe families love. But in this recipe, brought back from our archives, the salsa and seasonings give meat loaf a south-of-the-border flavor that's very yum! Round out the meal by serving it with cooked quinoa, couscous, or rice, and your favorite roasted or cooked veggies.

Salsa Meat Loaf

Prep Time: 15 Minutes
Start to Finish: 1 Hour
  15 Minutes
4 servings

1 lb ground beef or ground turkey (at least 80% lean)
½ cup quick-cooking oats
1 teaspoon dried basil leaves
½ teaspoon dried oregano leaves

¼ teaspoon salt, if desired
⅛ teaspoon pepper
½ cup chunky-style salsa
1 egg, slightly beaten
Additional salsa, if desired

1 Heat oven to 350°F.

2 In large bowl, mix all ingredients except additional salsa. Spread mixture in ungreased 8×4-inch loaf pan or shape into 8×4-inch loaf in ungreased 9-inch pan.

3 Insert ovenproof meat thermometer so tip is in center of loaf. Bake uncovered 50 to 60 minutes or until beef is no longer pink in center and thermometer reads 160°F; drain. Let stand 5 minutes; remove meat loaf from pan. Cut into slices. Serve with additional salsa.

1 Serving Calories 260; Total Fat 15g (Saturated Fat 5g, Trans Fat 0.5g); Cholesterol 115mg; Sodium 300mg; Total Carbohydrate 9g (Dietary Fiber 2g); Protein 23g **Carbohydrate Choices:** ½

From our *Bisquick Makes It Easy* magazine (1994), we love this cheesy herbed biscuit—topped spaghetti casserole for quick and hearty suppers.

Italian Bake

Prep Time: 20 Minutes
Start to Finish: 50 Minutes
8 servings

1½ lb ground beef
(at least 80% lean)

1½ cups sliced fresh
mushrooms (about 4 oz)

1 jar (24 oz) tomato pasta sauce

1 cup shredded mozzarella
cheese (4 oz)

2 cups Bisquick Original
Pancake & Baking Mix

1¼ cups milk

1 tablespoon vegetable oil

1 teaspoon dried oregano leaves

¼ cup grated Parmesan cheese

1 Heat oven to 375°F. Grease 13×9-inch baking dish with vegetable shortening or spray with cooking spray.

2 In 10-inch skillet, cook beef and mushrooms over medium heat 8 to 10 minutes, stirring occasionally, until beef is thoroughly cooked. Drain; return mixture to skillet. Stir in pasta sauce.

3 Spread in pan; sprinkle with mozzarella cheese. In medium bowl, stir together Bisquick mix, milk, oil, and oregano with spoon until blended (batter will be lumpy). Spoon evenly over ground beef mixture; sprinkle with Parmesan cheese.

4 Bake 28 to 30 minutes or until golden brown and bubbly around the edges.

1 Serving Calories 390; Total Fat 17g (Saturated Fat 7g, Trans Fat 0.5g); Cholesterol 65mg; Sodium 780mg; Total Carbohydrate 35g (Dietary Fiber 2g); Protein 24g **Carbohydrate Choices:** 2

Originally appearing in our 1992 *Easy Summer Get-Togethers* magazine, brisket was a huge hit for backyard barbecues. Its ridiculously easy prep and amazing flavor are perfect for hungry crowds. Check with the butcher at your supermarket ahead of time to be sure there will be one waiting for you when you want it.

Barbecue Beef Brisket

Prep Time: 10 Minutes
Start to Finish: 3 Hours
  10 Minutes
12 servings

4 to 5 lb fresh beef brisket
  (not corned beef)
1 teaspoon salt
½ cup ketchup
¼ cup white vinegar
1 tablespoon Worcestershire
  sauce

1½ teaspoons liquid smoke
¼ teaspoon pepper
1 small onion, finely chopped
  (about ½ cup)

1 Heat oven to 325°F.

2 Remove fat from beef. Rub surface of beef brisket with salt. Place in ungreased 13×9-inch pan. Mix remaining ingredients; pour over beef.

3 Cover and bake about 3 hours or until tender. Cover loosely; let stand 15 to 20 minutes before slicing.

4 To serve, cut beef across grain into thin slices; arrange on serving platter. Spoon any remaining juices in pan over sliced beef if desired.

Grilled Beef Brisket Barbecue: Heat gas or charcoal grill to medium for direct heat. After rubbing surface of beef with salt, place beef on 20×15-inch piece of heavy-duty aluminum foil. Mix remaining ingredients; pour over beef. Wrap securely in foil. Cover grill. Cook about 1½ hours, turning once, until tender.

Betty's Cooking Tip: The simple homemade barbecue sauce adds a smokiness from liquid smoke. You can find it near the seasonings in larger supermarkets or online. If you want extra sauce for serving with the meat, double the sauce portion of the recipe.

1 Serving Calories 230; Total Fat 10g (Saturated Fat 3.5g, Trans Fat 0g); Cholesterol 95mg; Sodium 350mg; Total Carbohydrate 4g (Dietary Fiber 0g); Protein 32g **Carbohydrate Choices:** 0

This slow-simmered stew debuted in *Betty Crocker's Buffets* cookbook (1984). It can be made in advance to add even more flavor and make it easy to serve to company. Paired with silky mashed potatoes, cooked egg noodles, or steaming-hot rice, it's a great winter dish everyone will love.

Beef Burgundy

Prep Time: 45 Minutes
Start to Finish: 2 Hours
   15 Minutes
8 servings

4 lb beef boneless round steak,
   1 inch thick
¼ cup vegetable shortening
3 medium onions, sliced

2 packages (8 oz each) sliced
   fresh mushrooms
3 tablespoons Gold Medal
   all-purpose flour
1½ teaspoons salt
¼ teaspoon dried marjoram
   leaves
¼ teaspoon dried thyme leaves
¼ teaspoon pepper

2 cups dry red wine or
   nonalcoholic wine
1 cup water
1 teaspoon roasted beef base
   (from 8-oz jar) or 1 beef
   bouillon cube

1 Cut beef into 1-inch cubes. In 5- or 6-quart Dutch oven, heat shortening over medium heat until hot. Add beef and cook, stirring occasionally, 10 to 15 minutes or until browned on all sides. Remove beef with slotted spoon to heatproof bowl; set aside.

2 Add onions and mushrooms to Dutch oven. Cook about 5 minutes, stirring frequently (if vegetables stick to the pan, add 1 tablespoon additional shortening), or until tender. Remove vegetables with slotted spoon to heatproof bowl. Let cool slightly; cover and refrigerate.

3 In same Dutch oven, mix beef, flour, salt, marjoram, thyme, and pepper. Stir in wine, water, and beef base. Heat to boiling; reduce heat. Cover and simmer about 1½ hours or until beef is fork tender (liquid should just cover beef throughout cooking).

4 Add vegetables to beef. Heat about 15 minutes, stirring occasionally, until hot.

Betty's Cooking Tip: If the liquid level gets low during cooking, so that it is no longer just covering the top of the beef, mix ⅔ cup additional wine with ⅓ cup additional water. Add just enough liquid to cover beef. Reserve any remaining liquid to continue to add if necessary.

Make-Ahead Directions: Prepare through Step 3; cool beef mixture 30 minutes at room temperature. Cover and refrigerate no longer than 24 hours. Continue as directed.

1 Serving Calories 410; Total Fat 15g (Saturated Fat 5g, Trans Fat 0g); Cholesterol 145mg; Sodium 680mg; Total Carbohydrate 8g (Dietary Fiber 1g); Protein 58g **Carbohydrate Choices:** ½

Betty Crocker's Buffets

Buffets

Menus, Recipes and Planning Tips
for Easy and Successful Home Entertaining

Betty Crocker's Buffets cookbook (1984) contained
"menus, recipes and planning tips for easy and
successful home entertaining" for dinners, late suppers,
breakfasts and brunches, and more.

There's actually no chicken in it! This Midwest and Southern favorite was said to have been created to use inexpensive cuts of beef that were pounded thin, dipped, and fried like fried chicken.

Parmesan Chicken-Fried Steak

Prep Time: 30 Minutes
Start to Finish: 30 Minutes
4 servings

STEAK
⅓ cup Gold Medal all-purpose flour

½ teaspoon salt

½ teaspoon garlic powder

¼ teaspoon pepper

⅓ cup milk

⅓ cup unseasoned dry bread crumbs

⅓ cup grated Parmesan cheese

½ teaspoon dried oregano leaves

1 lb boneless beef round steak, ½ inch thick

3 tablespoons vegetable oil

GRAVY
1 tablespoon butter

1 tablespoon Gold Medal all-purpose flour

1 cup half-and-half or milk

¼ teaspoon salt

¼ teaspoon coarsely ground black pepper

1 In shallow dish, mix ⅓ cup flour, ½ teaspoon salt, the garlic powder, and ¼ teaspoon pepper. Place milk in second shallow dish. In third shallow dish, mix bread crumbs, cheese, and oregano.

2 Cut steak into 4 pieces. To flatten each piece of steak, place between 2 pieces of plastic wrap or waxed paper. Working from center, gently pound steak with flat side of meat mallet or rolling pin until about ¼ inch thick; remove wrap.

3 Dip each steak piece in flour mixture to coat. Dip in milk; dip in bread crumb mixture to coat.

4 In 12-inch skillet, heat oil over medium heat until hot. Add steak; cook 10 to 15 minutes, turning once, or until tender. Remove steak from skillet; cover to keep warm.

5 In same skillet, melt butter. Stir in 1 tablespoon flour with whisk. Cook and stir until light brown. Add remaining gravy ingredients; cook and stir over medium heat until bubbly and thickened. Serve gravy over steak.

1 Serving Calories 470; Total Fat 28g (Saturated Fat 11g, Trans Fat 0.5g); Cholesterol 110mg; Sodium 790mg; Total Carbohydrate 21g (Dietary Fiber 1g); Protein 35g **Carbohydrate Choices:** 1½

Our food editor developed this recipe for *Betty Crocker's Pasta Cookbook* (1995) with her family in mind! It's a simple skillet meal, with the flavors her three boys loved, which could be made on busy nights of running them to their various activities.

Rigatoni–Smoked Bratwurst Skillet

Prep Time: 40 Minutes
Start to Finish: 40 Minutes
4 servings

1 cup water
1 can (14.5 oz) Italian-style diced tomatoes, undrained

1 can (6 oz) tomato paste
1 tablespoon sugar
½ teaspoon onion powder
¼ teaspoon salt
⅛ teaspoon pepper
1 cup small-curd cottage cheese

2 cups (6 oz) uncooked rigatoni pasta (from 16-oz box)
1 package (14 oz) fully cooked smoked bratwurst, kielbasa, or ring bologna, sliced
2 tablespoons chopped fresh parsley

1 In 10-inch skillet, mix water, tomatoes, tomato paste, sugar, onion powder, salt, and pepper. Heat to boiling. Stir in cottage cheese; heat to boiling.

2 Stir in rigatoni and bratwurst. Heat to boiling; reduce heat. Cover and simmer 25 to 30 minutes, stirring frequently, until rigatoni is tender. Uncover and simmer about 5 minutes or until desired consistency. Stir in parsley.

1 Serving Calories 630; Total Fat 30g (Saturated Fat 11g, Trans Fat 0g); Cholesterol 55mg; Sodium 1460mg; Total Carbohydrate 62g (Dietary Fiber 5g); Protein 27g **Carbohydrate Choices:** 4

From our *Mexican Fast & Flavorful* magazine (1994), we love this recipe for its simple prep and oh-so-yummy papaya salsa! It's such a great dish to wow your family and friends with.

Grilled Pork–Papaya Salsa Tacos

Prep Time: 20 Minutes
Start to Finish: 40 Minutes
4 servings (2 tacos each)

PAPAYA SALSA

1 teaspoon lime zest
1/4 cup fresh lime juice
2 tablespoons honey
1 1/2 teaspoons olive oil
1/8 teaspoon salt
1/8 teaspoon pepper
2 kiwifruit, peeled, diced
1 small papaya, peeled, seeded, and diced
1 jalapeño chile, seeded, chopped, if desired
2 teaspoons chopped fresh cilantro, if desired
1/4 cup diced red onion

TACOS

1 to 1 1/4 lb pork tenderloin, trimmed of fat
2 tablespoons olive oil
8 flour tortillas (8 to 10 inch), warmed
1 cup shredded Monterey Jack cheese (4 oz)

1 In medium bowl, mix lime zest, lime juice, honey, oil, salt, and pepper. Add remaining salsa ingredients; toss. Let stand while preparing tacos.

2 Heat gas or charcoal grill to medium for direct heat. Brush tenderloin with 2 tablespoons olive oil. Place pork on the grill. Cover grill; cook 10 minutes. Turn pork; grill 8 to 12 minutes longer or until instant-read thermometer inserted in center of tenderloin reads at least 145°F.

3 Transfer to cutting board; cover with foil and let stand 5 minutes. Cut tenderloin into slices with serrated knife.

4 Divide pork among tortillas, placing onto half of each tortilla; top with about 2 tablespoons of the cheese. Top with salsa. Fold tortilla in half over filling.

Skillet Pork–Papaya Salsa Tacos: Reduce olive oil for pork to 1 tablespoon. Cut tenderloin into 1/2-inch slices. In 12-inch nonstick skillet, heat olive oil over medium-high heat. Add pork; cook 5 to 7 minutes, turning once, until no longer pink in center. Remove pork from skillet to heatproof platter. Continue as directed in Step 4.

1 Serving Calories 710; Total Fat 30g (Saturated Fat 11g, Trans Fat 0g); Cholesterol 95mg; Sodium 1030mg; Total Carbohydrate 69g (Dietary Fiber 5g); Protein 41g **Carbohydrate Choices:** 4 1/2

Betty's Cooking Tip: While the cooked pork rests in Step 3, keep the grill on to warm the tortillas. Spread them out over the grill; let them cook about a minute or until warmed.

Make-Ahead Directions: The papaya salsa can be prepared up to 8 hours in advance. Cover and refrigerate until ready to serve. Serve cold or at room temperature.

This is from our *Meat and Potatoes* magazine (#109). Cream of mushroom soup has been used as a base for oodles of casseroles for decades. We love this recipe for its simplicity and combination of ingredients that still make it perfect for today's dinner table.

Pork Chop and New Potato Skillet

Prep Time: 25 Minutes
Start to Finish: 55 Minutes
6 servings

2 tablespoons butter

6 boneless pork loin or rib chops, ½ inch thick (about 1½ lb)

1½ cups sliced fresh mushrooms (about 4 oz)

1 can (10.5 oz) condensed cream of mushroom soup

¼ cup water

2 tablespoons dry white wine or apple juice

¾ teaspoon chopped fresh or ¼ teaspoon dried thyme leaves

½ teaspoon garlic powder

½ teaspoon Worcestershire sauce

6 medium new potatoes (about 1½ lb), cut lengthwise into fourths

1 tablespoon chopped pimiento

1 package (10 oz) frozen green peas

Pepper, if desired

1 In 12-inch nonstick skillet, melt 1 tablespoon of the butter over medium-high heat. Cook pork in butter until browned on both sides. Remove from skillet to heatproof plate; keep warm.

2 Reduce heat to medium. Heat remaining 1 tablespoon butter in same skillet until melted. Cook mushrooms in butter 3 minutes, stirring frequently, or until tender. Stir in soup, water, wine, thyme, garlic powder, and Worcestershire sauce. Return pork to skillet. Heat to boiling, stirring occasionally; reduce heat. Cover and simmer 15 minutes.

3 Add potatoes to skillet. Heat to boiling; reduce heat. Cover and simmer 15 minutes. Stir in pimiento and peas. Cover and simmer about 10 minutes, stirring occasionally, until instant-read meat thermometer reads at least 145°F and peas are tender. Sprinkle with pepper.

1 Serving Calories 420; Total Fat 20g (Saturated Fat 8g, Trans Fat 0g); Cholesterol 80mg; Sodium 480mg; Total Carbohydrate 30g (Dietary Fiber 4g); Protein 29g **Carbohydrate Choices:** 2

This tasty make-ahead sandwich is perfect for a picnic or backyard gathering. The secret to phenomenal flavor is to not skimp on the refrigeration steps. Allow the olive salad and then the sandwich its full time in the fridge so that the flavors have enough time to marry. Serve wedges with picks speared with additional marinated veggies and/or olives. Fun!

Muffuletta Sandwich

Prep Time: 15 Minutes
Start to Finish: 10 Hours
  15 Minutes
6 wedges

OLIVE SALAD

1/3 cup olive oil

1 anchovy fillet, mashed
  (1/2 teaspoon) or 1/2 teaspoon
  anchovy paste

1 large clove garlic, finely
  chopped

1/2 cup drained chopped
  pimiento-stuffed green olives

1/2 cup drained chopped pitted
  kalamata olives

1/2 cup drained chopped
  mixed pickled vegetables
  (from 16-oz jar)

2 tablespoons chopped fresh
  parsley

1/2 teaspoon dried oregano
  leaves

1/8 teaspoon pepper

SANDWICH

1 large (8- to 10-inch-diameter)
  unsliced round or oval loaf
  Italian or sourdough bread

1/2 lb thinly sliced Italian salami

1/3 lb thinly sliced provolone
  cheese

1/4 lb thinly sliced fully cooked
  smoked ham

1 In small glass bowl, place oil. Stir in anchovy and garlic until well blended. Stir in remaining olive salad ingredients. Cover and refrigerate, stirring occasionally, at least 8 hours but no longer than 24 hours to blend flavors.

2 Cut bread horizontally in half. Remove 1/2-inch layer of soft bread from inside each half to within 1/2 inch of edge. Reserve bread scraps for another use. Drain olive salad, reserving marinade. Brush reserved marinade over cut sides of bread. Layer salami, half of the olive salad, the cheese, ham, and remaining olive salad on bottom half of bread. Cover with top half of bread; press lightly.

3 Wrap sandwich tightly with plastic wrap. Refrigerate at least 2 hours or no longer than 24 hours. Cut into 6 wedges.

Betty's Cooking Tip: Pickled vegetables, also known as giardiniera, can be found near the pickles at many larger grocery stores.

1 Wedge Calories 440; Total Fat 36g (Saturated Fat 11g, Trans Fat 0g); Cholesterol 70mg; Sodium 1570mg; Total Carbohydrate 9g (Dietary Fiber 1g); Protein 20g **Carbohydrate Choices:** 1/2

Okay, this one was really a fun surprise in our testing. From *Bisquick Makes It Easy* magazine, we were blown away by the clever way to serve hot dogs and tasty flavor of the "bun." We had to include it in our book for all the hot dog lovers out there.

Mexican-Style Franks in a Loaf

Prep Time: 15 Minutes
Start to Finish: 40 Minutes
6 servings

1½ cups Bisquick Original Pancake & Baking Mix
½ cup shredded cheddar cheese (2 oz)
¾ cup chunky-style salsa

¼ cup milk
1 egg
6 hot dogs

1 Heat oven to 400°F. Grease 9×5-inch loaf pan with vegetable shortening or spray with cooking spray.

2 In medium bowl, stir together Bisquick mix, ¼ cup of the cheese, ¼ cup of the salsa, the milk, and egg with spoon until blended. Spread in pan. Arrange hot dogs crosswise on dough in pan, curving slightly and pressing to fit pan and into dough just enough to partially cover the hot dogs.

3 Bake 15 to 20 minutes or until toothpick inserted into the biscuit portion comes out clean. Sprinkle with remaining ¼ cup cheese. Bake an additional 1 to 2 minutes or until cheese is melted. To serve, cut bread between hot dogs; serve with remaining ½ cup salsa.

November 1994 #98
Betty Crocker
Easy Main Dishes
Ready-To-Cook In 15 MINUTES

Bisquick
Makes it Easy!

NEW!
PIZZAS, CASSEROLES, PANCAKES & MORE!!

1 Serving Calories 310; Total Fat 17g (Saturated Fat 6g, Trans Fat 0g); Cholesterol 80mg; Sodium 1000mg; Total Carbohydrate 29g (Dietary Fiber 1g); Protein 10g
Carbohydrate Choices: 2

Betty Crocker Creative Recipes—nearly 300 magazines published between 1983 and 2014. These digest-size cookbooks were available near grocery store checkouts across the US and Canada. Many can still be found online today.

Could it be true? Can a recipe that only takes 10 minutes to prep really deliver on homemade taste? The answer is yes! A flavor-packed marinade/sauce elevates this fast recipe to company-worthy status. Serve it with the rice so you don't miss a single drop of the sauce.

Margarita Shrimp

Prep Time: 10 Minutes
Start to Finish: 55 Minutes
6 servings

MARINADE

¼ cup tequila
¼ cup red wine vinegar
2 tablespoons vegetable oil
2 tablespoons fresh lime juice

1 teaspoon ground red pepper
(cayenne)
½ teaspoon salt
2 cloves garlic, finely chopped
1 medium red bell pepper,
finely chopped (about 1 cup)

SHRIMP

24 uncooked extra-large
(16 to 20 count) shrimp,

peeled (with tails left on),
deveined (about 1½ lb)
4 (10- to 12-inch) metal skewers

SERVE WITH

Cooked white or brown rice,
if desired
Sliced green onions and lime
wedges, if desired

1 In shallow glass or plastic dish, mix all marinade ingredients. Stir in shrimp. Cover and refrigerate 30 minutes.

2 Heat gas or charcoal grill to medium for direct heat.

3 Remove shrimp from marinade; reserving marinade. On each skewer, thread 6 shrimp. Place kabobs on grill.

4 Cover grill; cook shrimp 4 to 6 minutes, turning and brushing once with marinade, until pink.

5 In 1-quart nonaluminum saucepan, heat reserved marinade to boiling; reduce heat. Simmer uncovered over low heat about 5 minutes or until bell pepper is tender. Serve shrimp with rice and marinade; garnish with green onions and lime wedges.

1 Serving Calories 90; Total Fat 5g (Saturated Fat 1g, Trans Fat 0g); Cholesterol 65mg; Sodium 240mg; Total Carbohydrate 2g (Dietary Fiber 0g); Protein 8g **Carbohydrate Choices:** 0

{ pictured on the next page }

Betty Crocker Gold Medal Flour Home Service Talks ad.

Betty Crocker's first radio show, Gold Medal Flour Home Service Talks, was broadcast across Minnesota, and was the predecessor to the Betty Crocker Cooking School of the Air national radio program.

This is such a delightful way to enjoy tuna! On the table in 30 minutes, we love the warm and cheesy goodness you get from this large baked sandwich. What a weeknight winner!

Family-Size Tuna Melt

Prep Time: 15 Minutes
Start to Finish: 30 Minutes
4 servings (2 pieces each)

2 cups Bisquick Original Pancake & Baking Mix
½ cup mayonnaise or salad dressing

⅓ cup milk
1 can (12 oz) chunk light tuna in water, drained, flaked
1 medium stalk celery, finely chopped (½ cup)
⅓ cup mayonnaise or salad dressing

2 tablespoons sweet pickle relish
6 slices (½ oz each) American cheese
Chopped parsley, if desired

1 Heat oven to 450°F. Grease cookie sheet with vegetable shortening or spray with cooking spray.

2 In medium bowl, stir together Bisquick mix, ½ cup mayonnaise, and the milk with spoon; beat 30 seconds. On cookie sheet, pat dough into 12×8-inch rectangle. Press the edges with the tines of a fork, if desired.

3 Bake about 6 minutes or until edges just start to brown. Meanwhile, in medium bowl, mix remaining ingredients except cheese and parsley.

4 Spread tuna mixture over hot rectangle. Top with cheese slices. Bake about 5 minutes longer or until filling is hot and cheese is melted. Sprinkle with parsley. Let stand 2 minutes before cutting. Cut into 2 rows by 4 rows.

1 Serving Calories 700; Total Fat 44g (Saturated Fat 10g, Trans Fat 0g); Cholesterol 70mg; Sodium 1490mg; Total Carbohydrate 50g (Dietary Fiber 1g); Protein 24g **Carbohydrate Choices:** 3

This is a refreshing yet filling salad to serve on a hot summer day, from our *Bravo! Pasta* magazine (1993). If you're a shrimp lover, double the shrimp and omit the imitation crab. Or if you love crab, double the imitation crab and omit the shrimp!

Seafood Pasta Salad with Ginger Dressing

Prep Time: 15 Minutes
Start to Finish: 2 Hours 15 Minutes
12 servings

GINGER DRESSING
⅔ cup mayonnaise or salad dressing
⅔ cup plain nonfat Greek yogurt
2 tablespoons soy sauce
2 teaspoons sugar
1 teaspoon ground ginger
Dash red pepper sauce

SALAD
1 package (16 oz) spaghetti
1 package (8 oz) refrigerated chunk-style imitation crabmeat
1 package (16 oz) frozen cooked deveined peeled medium shrimp (31 to 40 count), thawed
1 cup coarsely chopped jicama or 2 cans (8 oz each) sliced water chestnuts, drained
½ cup chopped fresh cilantro leaves or parsley
2 medium cucumbers, peeled if desired, cut in half lengthwise, and sliced ¼ inch thick
1 medium carrot, shredded (1 cup)
Leaf lettuce, if desired

1 In medium bowl, mix all dressing ingredients. Cover and refrigerate 2 hours to blend flavors.

2 Break spaghetti in half. Cook and drain as directed on package. Rinse with cold water; drain again. In large bowl, mix spaghetti with remaining salad ingredients except leaf lettuce. Toss with dressing. Serve on lettuce.

1 Serving Calories 320; Total Fat 11g (Saturated Fat 2g, Trans Fat 0g); Cholesterol 70mg; Sodium 660mg; Total Carbohydrate 39g (Dietary Fiber 3g); Protein 17g **Carbohydrate Choices:** 2½

From *Betty Crocker's Pasta Cookbook* (1995), this flavorful dish is fancy enough for guests but easy enough for weeknight meals. It's got that great supper club vibe. The original recipe included directions for making your own ravioli. We've simplified it for a quick weeknight meal.

Ravioli with Roasted Red Pepper Cream

Prep Time: 15 Minutes
Start to Finish: 25 Minutes
6 servings

1 jar (7 oz) roasted red bell peppers, undrained

¼ cup chopped onion

1 cup heavy whipping cream or half-and-half

1 tablespoon chopped fresh or 1 teaspoon dried basil leaves

¼ teaspoon coarsely ground black pepper

2 packages (9 oz each) refrigerated cheese ravioli

¼ cup shredded Parmesan cheese

½ cup chopped walnuts

Additional chopped fresh basil leaves, if desired

1 In 1-quart saucepan, heat roasted peppers and onion to boiling; reduce heat. Simmer uncovered about 5 minutes, stirring occasionally, or until onion is soft. Remove from heat. Using immersion blender, blend until smooth. (Or carefully pour into blender container. Cover and blend on high speed until smooth; pour back into saucepan.)

2 Stir in whipping cream, basil, and pepper. Cook over low heat, stirring occasionally, just until hot; remove from heat; cover and keep warm.

3 Cook and drain ravioli as directed on package. On platter or serving plates, place ravioli. Spoon sauce over ravioli; sprinkle with Parmesan cheese, walnuts, and additional chopped fresh basil leaves.

1 Serving Calories 350; Total Fat 25g (Saturated Fat 12g, Trans Fat 0.5g); Cholesterol 125mg; Sodium 760mg; Total Carbohydrate 23g (Dietary Fiber 1g); Protein 10g **Carbohydrate Choices:** 1½

Betty Crocker's Pasta Cookbook (1995) shared,
in easy steps, how to make your own pastas
and had recipes ranging from appetizers to
main dishes, meatless recipes, and salads.

From our 1979 cookbook, *Century of Success*, this easy and comforting casserole is still a winner today, being meatless, hearty, and inexpensive to prepare!

Three Bean and Cornbread Casserole

Prep Time: 15 Minutes
Start to Finish: 45 Minutes
8 servings

BEAN MIXTURE

2 cans (28 oz each) baked beans

1 can (15.5 oz) kidney beans, drained

1 can (15.25 to 15.5 oz) cannellini or lima beans, drained

1 can (8 oz) tomato sauce

1/3 cup ketchup

1/4 cup finely chopped onion

2 tablespoons packed brown sugar

1/2 teaspoon salt

1/2 teaspoon dry mustard

1/4 teaspoon pepper

CORNBREAD TOPPING

2/3 cup Gold Medal all-purpose flour

1/3 cup yellow cornmeal

1 tablespoon granulated sugar

1 teaspoon baking powder

1/2 teaspoon salt

1/2 cup milk

2 tablespoons butter, softened

1 egg

1 Heat oven to 425°F.

2 In large bowl, mix all bean mixture ingredients. Pour into ungreased 13×9-inch (3-quart) glass baking dish.

3 In medium bowl, mix all cornbread topping ingredients with whisk until smooth; spoon evenly over bean mixture to within 1 inch of edges.

4 Bake 25 to 30 minutes until topping is golden brown.

1 Serving Calories 430; Total Fat 6g (Saturated Fat 3g, Trans Fat 0g); Cholesterol 45mg; Sodium 1670mg; Total Carbohydrate 75g (Dietary Fiber 16g); Protein 18g **Carbohydrate Choices:** 5

A French dish consisting of white beans cooked slowly with various meats, the resulting casserole is a welcome dinner on a cold night. Our version comes together quickly for you to pop in the oven. Then wait for the delicious aroma to fill your kitchen, beckoning your family to the table without saying a word.

Everyday Cassoulet

Prep Time: 20 Minutes
Start to Finish: 1 Hour 30 Minutes
8 servings

1 lb Polish or smoked sausage, cut diagonally into 1-inch pieces

1 can (15 to 16 oz) great northern beans, drained, rinsed

1 can (15 to 16 oz) kidney beans, drained, rinsed

1 can (15 oz) black beans, drained, rinsed

1 can (15 oz) tomato sauce

3 medium carrots, thinly sliced (1½ cups)

2 small onions, thinly sliced, separated into rings

2 cloves garlic, finely chopped

½ cup dry red wine or beef broth

2 tablespoons packed brown sugar

2 tablespoons chopped fresh or 1½ teaspoons dried thyme leaves

1 Heat oven to 375°F. In ungreased 3-quart casserole, mix all ingredients.

2 Cover and bake 1 hour to 1 hour 10 minutes or until mixture is hot and bubbly and carrots are tender.

Lighter Everyday Cassoulet: Substitute turkey smoked sausage for the smoked sausage.

1 Serving Calories 400; Total Fat 17g (Saturated Fat 6g, Trans Fat 0g); Cholesterol 45mg; Sodium 1010mg; Total Carbohydrate 39g (Dietary Fiber 10g); Protein 20g **Carbohydrate Choices:** 2½

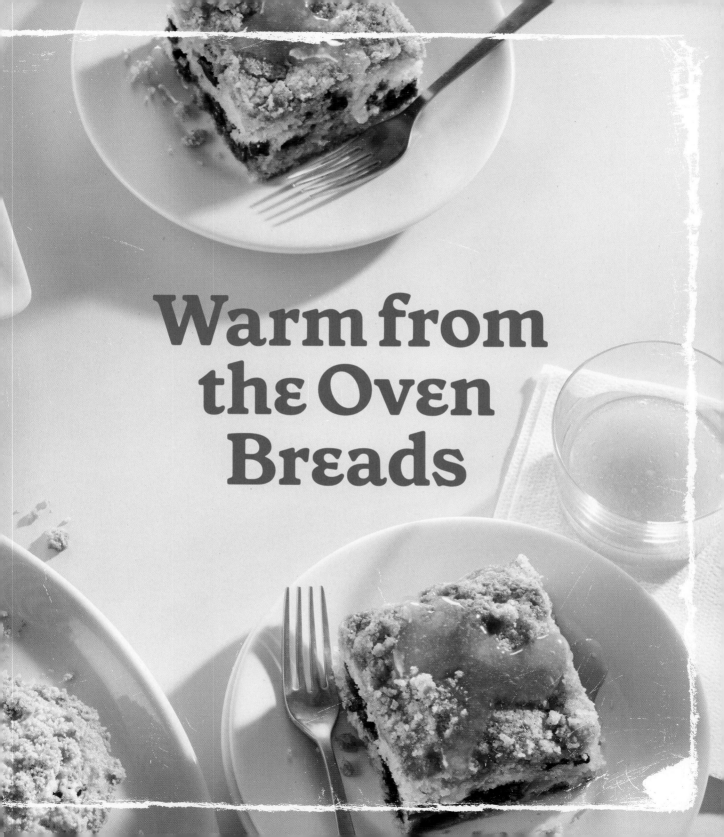

Warm from the Oven Breads

These delicious muffins still bowl us over with their combination of oats, two kinds of flour, spices, and dried cherries. Serve them with softened butter and jam alongside a cup of coffee or tea.

Oatmeal-Cherry Muffins

Prep Time: 15 Minutes
Start to Finish: 35 Minutes
12 muffins

1 cup buttermilk
1 cup old-fashioned oats

½ cup packed brown sugar
⅓ cup butter, melted
2 teaspoons orange zest
1 egg
½ cup Gold Medal
   all-purpose flour

½ cup Gold Medal whole
   wheat flour
1½ teaspoons baking powder
1 teaspoon salt
1 teaspoon ground cinnamon
1 cup coarsely chopped dried
   cherries

1 Heat oven to 400°F. In small bowl, pour buttermilk over oats. Grease bottoms of 12 regular-size muffin cups with vegetable shortening, spray with cooking spray, or line with paper baking cups.

2 In large bowl, mix brown sugar, melted butter, orange zest, and egg with spoon. Stir in both types of flour, baking powder, salt, and cinnamon just until flour is moistened. Stir in oat mixture; fold in cherries. Fill muffin cups three-quarters full.

3 Bake 15 to 20 minutes or until golden brown and toothpick inserted in center comes out clean. Immediately remove from pan to cooling rack. Serve warm if desired.

Betty's Cooking Tip: Whole wheat flour adds extra nutrition and fiber to these muffins. If you wish, you could just use 1 cup of all-purpose flour instead of using both types.

Betty's Cooking Tip: Don't have buttermilk on hand? Simply measure 2 tablespoons of regular white vinegar into a measuring cup. Add enough milk to equal 1 cup. Let stand for a minute for the milk to "sour" and use as directed in Step 1.

1 Muffin Calories 210; Total Fat 7g (Saturated Fat 3.5g, Trans Fat 0g); Cholesterol 30mg; Sodium 330mg; Total Carbohydrate 34g (Dietary Fiber 2g); Protein 4g **Carbohydrate Choices:** 2

The *Betty Crocker Picture Cook Book* (1950) was a first of its kind and started a nearly 75-year tradition of publishing culturally relevant cookbooks of the times. To date, nearly 300 cookbook titles have been published.

From our *Holiday Baking* magazine (1997), these delicious muffins have a streusel topping that makes them extra special any time of year.

Cranberry Orange Streusel Muffins

Prep Time: 15 Minutes
Start to Finish: 40 Minutes
12 muffins

STREUSEL TOPPING
½ cup Gold Medal all-purpose flour
2 tablespoons packed brown sugar
¼ teaspoon ground cinnamon
2 tablespoons cold butter

MUFFINS
1 cup milk
¼ cup vegetable oil
½ teaspoon vanilla
1 egg
1 tablespoon orange zest
2 cups Gold Medal all-purpose or whole wheat flour
⅓ cup sugar
3 teaspoons baking powder
½ teaspoon salt
1 cup fresh cranberries, cut in half

1 Heat oven to 400°F. Grease bottoms only of 12 regular-size muffin cups with shortening, spray with cooking spray, or line with paper baking cups.

2 In small bowl, mix ½ cup flour, brown sugar, and cinnamon. Cut in butter with a fork until crumbly; set aside.

3 In large bowl, mix milk, oil, vanilla, egg, and orange zest until well mixed. Add 2 cups flour, the sugar, baking powder, and salt; stir just until flour is moistened (batter will be lumpy). Fold in cranberries. Divide batter evenly among muffin cups; sprinkle each with about 2 teaspoons streusel.

4 Bake 20 to 25 minutes or until golden brown. Immediately remove from pan to cooling rack. Serve warm or cool.

1 Muffin Calories 210; Total Fat 8g (Saturated Fat 2.5g, Trans Fat 0g); Cholesterol 20mg; Sodium 250mg; Total Carbohydrate 30g (Dietary Fiber 1g); Protein 4g **Carbohydrate Choices:** 2

From *Betty Crocker's Soups and Breads* magazine, these decadent muffins have a surprise inside—creme-filled sandwich cookies. So, we're saying yes—you can eat cookies for breakfast!

Chocolate Cookie Muffins

Prep Time: 15 Minutes
Start to Finish: 40 Minutes
12 muffins

MUFFINS

1⅔ cups Gold Medal all-purpose flour

½ cup unsweetened baking cocoa

1 teaspoon baking soda

1 teaspoon salt

¾ cup buttermilk

½ cup vegetable oil

½ cup packed brown sugar

1 teaspoon vanilla

1 egg

1 cup miniature creme-filled chocolate sandwich cookies or 1 cup coarsely chopped regular-size creme-filled chocolate sandwich cookies

GLAZE

½ cup powdered sugar

¼ teaspoon vanilla

2 to 3 teaspoons milk

1 Heat oven to 400°F. Grease bottoms only of 12 regular-size muffin cups with vegetable shortening, spray with cooking spray, or line with paper baking cups.

2 In large bowl, mix flour, cocoa, baking soda, and salt. In small bowl, mix buttermilk, oil, brown sugar, 1 teaspoon vanilla, and egg with fork or whisk. Stir buttermilk mixture into flour mixture just until flour is moistened (batter will be lumpy). Fold in cookies. Divide evenly among muffin cups.

3 Bake 13 to 16 minutes or until toothpick inserted in center comes out clean. Remove from pan to wire rack. Cool 5 minutes.

4 Meanwhile, in small bowl, stir powdered sugar, ¼ teaspoon vanilla, and enough milk until smooth and thin enough to drizzle.

5 Drizzle glaze over muffins. Serve warm if desired.

1 Muffin Calories 280; Total Fat 12g (Saturated Fat 2.5g, Trans Fat 0g); Cholesterol 15mg; Sodium 360mg; Total Carbohydrate 37g (Dietary Fiber 2g); Protein 4g **Carbohydrate Choices:** 2½

From *Betty Crocker's Classics Recipe Cards*, the introduction to the recipe read, "The name means 'little muffs,' to warm the fingers." These adorable little muffins are served upside down. We loved the fresh orange and honey flavor when we tested them.

Orange Honey Muffins

Prep Time: 15 Minutes
Start to Finish: 45 Minutes
12 muffins

12 teaspoons honey
3 slices orange, cut into fourths

1½ cups Gold Medal
   all-purpose flour
½ cup sugar
2 teaspoons baking powder
½ teaspoon salt
½ cup milk

¼ cup butter, softened
2 eggs
Additional butter and jam,
   marmalade, or additional
   honey, if desired

1 Heat oven to 400°F. Generously grease 12 regular-size muffin cups, spray with cooking spray, or line with foil-lined baking cups.

2 Spoon 1 teaspoon honey into each muffin cup; top with orange slice quarter.

3 In large bowl, mix flour, sugar, baking powder, and salt. Add remaining ingredients; mix just until dry ingredients are moistened (batter will look lumpy). Fill muffin cups about two-thirds full.

4 Bake 17 to 22 minutes or until golden brown and toothpick inserted in center comes out clean. Let stand about 5 minutes in pan. Gently loosen muffins with metal spatula; invert muffin pan onto cooling rack to remove muffins. Serve warm with additional butter.

Blueberry–Maple Muffins: Omit honey and orange slices. Fold in 1 cup fresh or frozen (do not thaw) blueberries and 1 teaspoon maple flavor before baking.

1 Muffin Calories 170; Total Fat 5g (Saturated Fat 3g, Trans Fat 0g); Cholesterol 40mg; Sodium 230mg; Total Carbohydrate 27g (Dietary Fiber 0g); Protein 3g
Carbohydrate Choices: 2

The Betty Crocker Recipe Card Library and Betty Crocker's Classics offered recipes in recipe boxes rather than a cookbook format.

We scoured our cookbooks and cooking magazines to see if we had any muffins with both corn and oatmeal, like Melinda G. described, but nothing surfaced. So, we accepted the challenge of re-creating them. We were surprised to find these tasty little gems versatile enough to go from the breakfast table to the dinner table; they would also be a terrific bread at any holiday meal. We see now why they are truly special!

Corn-Oatmeal Muffins

Prep Time: 15 Minutes
Start to Finish: 45 Minutes
12 muffins

1 cup quick-cooking oats
1 cup buttermilk
½ cup packed brown sugar
¼ cup butter, melted
1 egg
1 cup frozen whole kernel corn

1 cup Gold Medal
   all-purpose flour
1 teaspoon baking powder
½ teaspoon baking soda
½ teaspoon salt
Coarse sugar, if desired

1 Heat oven to 400°F. Grease bottoms only of 12 regular-size muffin cups with shortening, spray with cooking spray, or line with paper baking cups.

2 In medium bowl, stir oats and buttermilk until well mixed; let stand 5 minutes. Add brown sugar, melted butter, and egg; stir until well mixed. Stir in corn. Stir in flour, baking powder, baking soda, and salt all at once just until flour is moistened (batter will be lumpy). Divide batter evenly among muffin cups; sprinkle with coarse sugar.

3 Bake 17 to 21 minutes or until toothpick inserted in center comes out clean. For muffins baked in greased pan: let stand about 5 minutes in pan. Loosen top edges of muffins with metal spatula. Remove from pan to cooling rack; for muffins baked in paper baking cups: immediately remove from pan to cooling rack. Serve warm.

Kitchen Notes: This unique muffin is a little sweet, a little savory. We thought it would be fantastic served with jalapeño jelly or softened butter and honey.

1 Muffin Calories 160; Total Fat 5g (Saturated Fat 3g, Trans Fat 0g); Cholesterol 25mg; Sodium 250mg; Total Carbohydrate 25g (Dietary Fiber 1g); Protein 3g **Carbohydrate Choices:** 1½

Lost Recipe
Memory
"Best muffins ever."
—Melinda G.

This vintage classic, with the flavors of apple and spice, offers a nice change from banana bread. It keeps well in the refrigerator or freezer to have on hand when the craving strikes.

Apple-Raisin Bread

Prep Time: 15 Minutes
Start to Finish: 3 Hours 35 Minutes
2 loaves (12 slices each)

3 cups chopped unpeeled apples (about 3 medium)
3 cups Gold Medal all-purpose flour
2½ cups sugar
1¼ cups vegetable oil
⅔ cup raisins
½ cup chopped nuts

1 tablespoon plus 1 teaspoon vanilla
2 teaspoons ground cinnamon
1½ teaspoons salt
1½ teaspoons baking soda
1 teaspoon ground cloves
½ teaspoon baking powder
4 eggs, beaten

1 Heat oven to 325°F. Generously grease bottoms only of two 9×5-inch loaf pans with vegetable shortening or spray with cooking spray.

2 In large bowl, beat all ingredients with electric mixer on low speed, scraping bowl constantly, 1 minute. Beat on medium speed 1 minute. Pour into pans.

3 Bake about 1 hour or until toothpick inserted in center comes out clean. Cool 10 minutes in pans on cooling rack.

4 Loosen sides of loaves from pans; remove pans and place loaves top side up on cooling rack. Cool completely, about 2 hours, before slicing. Wrap tightly and store at room temperature up to 4 days or refrigerate up to 10 days.

Apple-Raisin Bread with Maple Drizzle:
In small bowl, mix 1 cup powdered sugar, 1 tablespoon milk, and 1 teaspoon maple-flavored syrup until smooth. Add additional milk, 1 teaspoon at a time, until smooth and drizzling consistency. Drizzle over tops of cooled loaves. Let stand until set before slicing.

Make-Ahead Directions: Store completely cooled, tightly wrapped bread in resealable freezer plastic bags up to 3 months. To thaw, loosen wrap and let stand at room temperature 2 to 3 hours.

1 Slice Calories 300; Total Fat 14g (Saturated Fat 2g, Trans Fat 0g); Cholesterol 30mg; Sodium 250mg; Total Carbohydrate 39g (Dietary Fiber 1g); Protein 3g **Carbohydrate Choices:** 2½

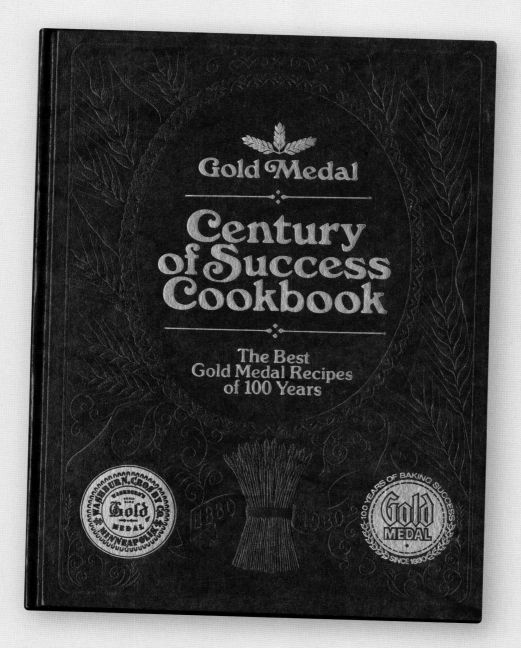

Gold Medal flour, the original product of the Washburn-Crosby Company, which was the predecessor of General Mills, was responsible for the ad that launched Betty Crocker. *Gold Medal Century of Success Cookbook* is a beloved book, chock-full of recipes developed in the Betty Crocker Kitchens, celebrating Gold Medal's 100 years of delicious eating.

From our *Baking for Today* cookbook, this delicious bread will win over any lemon lover.
With lemon in both the bread and glaze, it's a wonderful recipe to serve for breakfast, brunch, or even dessert.

Luscious Lemon Loaf

Prep Time: 20 Minutes
Start to Finish: 2 Hours
   35 Minutes
1 loaf (12 slices)

BREAD
1¾ cups Gold Medal
   all-purpose flour

½ teaspoon baking soda
¼ teaspoon salt
1 cup granulated sugar
½ cup butter, softened
2 eggs
½ cup sour cream
2 tablespoons lemon zest
¼ cup fresh lemon juice

LEMON GLAZE
½ cup powdered sugar
1 teaspoon lemon zest
1 to 2 tablespoons fresh
   lemon juice
Additional lemon zest,
   if desired

1 Heat oven to 325°F. Grease bottom only of 8×4-inch or 9×5-inch loaf pan with vegetable shortening or spray with cooking spray.

2 In small bowl, mix flour, baking soda, and salt; set aside. In large bowl, beat sugar and butter with electric mixer on medium speed, scraping bowl occasionally, until fluffy. Beat in eggs, sour cream, 2 tablespoons lemon zest, and ¼ cup lemon juice until well blended. Gradually beat in flour mixture until blended. Pour batter into pan.

3 Bake 55 to 65 minutes or until toothpick inserted in center comes out clean. Cool 10 minutes. Loosen sides of loaf from pan; remove from pan to wire rack. Cool completely, about 1 hour.

4 In small bowl, mix powdered sugar, 1 teaspoon lemon zest, and 1 tablespoon of lemon juice until smooth. Stir in additional lemon juice, 1 teaspoon at a time, until drizzling consistency. Drizzle over top of loaf, allowing some to drizzle down sides. Sprinkle with additional lemon zest. Let stand until glaze is set before slicing.

Betty's Cooking Tip: It's easier to zest lemons before juicing them, so we always try to call for zest before juice in our recipes, if we can. To get the most juice possible from lemons, roll them on the counter with the palm of your hand using a little pressure. Usually, you can get about 2 tablespoons juice from 1 lemon.

1 Slice Calories 260; Total Fat 11g (Saturated Fat 6g, Trans Fat 0g); Cholesterol 55mg; Sodium 180mg; Total Carbohydrate 37g (Dietary Fiber 0g); Protein 3g **Carbohydrate Choices:** 2½

We're suckers for a great quick bread. This one, from *Betty Crocker's Soups and Breads* magazine, caught our eye with the unusual combination of mandarin oranges and toffee bits. We whipped it up in the Test Kitchens and were very taken with the moist orange bread and toffee combination. It's a winner in our book.

Toffee-Orange Bread

Prep Time: 15 Minutes
Start to Finish: 3 Hours
50 Minutes
2 loaves (12 slices each)

1 jar (23.5 oz) mandarin oranges
in light syrup, drained,
1/2 cup syrup reserved

1 cup sugar
1/3 cup vegetable oil
1/4 cup milk
2 teaspoons orange zest
1 1/2 teaspoons vanilla
2 eggs

3 cups Gold Medal
all-purpose flour
2 teaspoons baking powder
1 teaspoon salt
1/4 teaspoon baking soda
3/4 cup toffee bits
(from 8-oz pkg)

1 Heat oven to 400°F. Grease bottoms only of two 8×4-inch or 9×5-inch loaf pans with vegetable shortening or spray with cooking spray.

2 Cut orange segments in half. In large bowl, beat reserved orange syrup, sugar, oil, milk, orange zest, vanilla, and eggs with fork. Stir in flour, baking powder, salt, and baking soda just until flour is moistened. Fold in oranges and 1/2 cup of the toffee bits.

3 Divide batter evenly between pans. Sprinkle with remaining 1/4 cup toffee bits.

4 Bake 8-inch loaves 50 to 60 minutes, 9-inch loaves 1 hour 15 minutes to 1 hour 25 minutes, or until toothpick inserted in center comes out clean. Cool 10 minutes in pans on cooling rack. Loosen sides of loaves from pans; remove from pans and place top side up on cooling rack.

5 Cool completely, about 2 hours, before slicing. Wrap tightly and store at room temperature up to 2 days or refrigerate up to 4 days.

Make-Ahead Directions: Store completely cooled, tightly wrapped bread in resealable freezer plastic bags up to 3 months. To thaw, loosen wrap and let stand at room temperature 2 to 3 hours.

1 Slice Calories 180; Total Fat 6g (Saturated Fat 2g, Trans Fat 0g); Cholesterol 15mg; Sodium 180mg; Total Carbohydrate 27g (Dietary Fiber 0g); Protein 2g **Carbohydrate Choices:** 2

A buckle is an old American term for a simple, single-layer cake made with blueberries or other berries. This pineapple-blueberry version serves equally well as a brunch coffee cake or dessert . . . or better yet . . . both!

Blueberry-Pineapple Buckle

Prep Time: 20 Minutes
Start to Finish: 1 Hour
   10 Minutes
9 servings

CAKE
1 can (8 oz) crushed pineapple
   in syrup, undrained
1¼ cups Gold Medal
   all-purpose flour
½ cup granulated sugar
¼ cup butter, softened

¼ cup shortening
½ cup milk
1½ teaspoons baking powder
1 teaspoon lemon zest, if desired
½ teaspoon vanilla
¼ teaspoon salt
1 egg
1 cup blueberries, fresh
   or frozen

CRUMB TOPPING
½ cup granulated sugar
⅓ cup Gold Medal
   all-purpose flour
¼ cup butter, softened
½ teaspoon ground cinnamon

PINEAPPLE SAUCE
2 tablespoons packed
   brown sugar
1 teaspoon cornstarch
¼ teaspoon fresh lemon juice

1 Heat oven to 350°F.

2 Drain pineapple, reserving syrup for pineapple sauce.

3 In large bowl, mix flour, ½ cup granulated sugar, ¼ cup butter, the shortening, milk, baking powder, lemon zest, vanilla, salt, and egg with spoon. Fold in blueberries and pineapple.

4 In ungreased 8-inch square pan, spread batter. In small bowl, mix all crumb topping ingredients until crumbly; sprinkle over batter.

5 Bake 45 to 50 minutes or until golden brown and toothpick inserted in center comes out clean.

6 Meanwhile, in 1-quart saucepan, mix brown sugar and cornstarch. Add enough water to reserved pineapple syrup to measure ⅔ cup; stir into brown sugar mixture. Cook over medium heat, stirring constantly, until mixture boils. Boil and stir 1 minute; remove from heat. Stir in lemon juice. Serve warm with warm buckle.

1 Serving Calories 370; Total Fat 17g (Saturated Fat 8g, Trans Fat 0g); Cholesterol 50mg; Sodium 240mg; Total Carbohydrate 50g (Dietary Fiber 1g); Protein 3g **Carbohydrate Choices:** 3

In the early days, home economists in the Betty Crocker Kitchens hosted tours for everyone, including school groups, youth organizations, dignitaries, and movie stars, in addition to their other responsibilities. "Proof positive that ten-year-olds can bake with Bisquick. These six Girl Scouts baked all 12 recipes suggested on the Bisquick package—and did a good job of it—in the Betty Crocker Kitchens in Minneapolis." (Copyright 1951, General Mills, Inc., Minneapolis, Minnesota. The Modern Millwheel, March 1951)

These pancakes are like the cousin of Belgian waffles. These were touted as "the most elegant pancakes you've ever tested or that we've discovered in years of testing" when they appeared in *Betty Crocker's Classics Recipe Cards*. They are lighter and fluffier than regular pancakes.

Fluffy Buttermilk Pancakes

Prep Time: 30 Minutes
Start to Finish: 30 Minutes
4 servings (3 pancakes each)

1½ cups Gold Medal
   all-purpose flour
1 tablespoon sugar
1 teaspoon baking powder
½ teaspoon salt
3 eggs, separated

1⅔ cups buttermilk
1 teaspoon baking soda
3 tablespoons butter, melted
Maple-flavored syrup and
   chopped strawberries, if
   desired

1 In small bowl, mix flour, sugar, baking powder, and salt; set aside. In medium bowl, beat egg yolks with whisk until fluffy. Stir in buttermilk and baking soda until well blended. Stir in melted butter. Stir in flour mixture just until moistened.

2 Place egg whites in medium bowl. Beat with electric mixer on high until stiff peaks form. Fold flour mixture gently into egg whites.

3 Heat griddle or skillet over medium heat or to 350°F. (To test griddle, sprinkle with a few drops of water. If bubbles jump around, heat is just right.) Brush with vegetable oil if necessary.

4 For each pancake, pour about ⅓ cup batter onto hot griddle. Cook 2 to 3 minutes or until bubbly on top and dry around edges. Flip; cook other side until golden brown. Serve with syrup and strawberries.

1 Serving Calories 380; Total Fat 16g (Saturated Fat 9g, Trans Fat 0g); Cholesterol 175mg; Sodium 950mg; Total Carbohydrate 45g (Dietary Fiber 1g); Protein 13g **Carbohydrate Choices:** 3

Scones have been around since the early 1800s or even earlier, by some accounts. Across the pond, they show up, especially with afternoon tea—frequently served with clotted cream and jam. They are so simple to make and offer a terrific combination of flavor and texture. What a wonderful addition to breakfast or as a companion to a cup of hot coffee.

Lemon-Currant Scones

Prep Time: 15 Minutes
Start to Finish: 30 Minutes
8 scones

2 cups Gold Medal all-purpose flour
¼ cup sugar
3 teaspoons baking powder
2 teaspoons lemon zest
¼ teaspoon salt

⅓ cup cold butter, cut into 8 pieces
⅓ cup dried currants
¾ to 1 cup milk
1 teaspoon sugar, if desired
Softened butter and/or honey, if desired

1 Heat oven to 425°F.

2 In large bowl, mix flour, ¼ cup sugar, the baking powder, lemon zest, and salt. Cut in butter, using pastry blender or fork, until mixture looks like fine crumbs. Stir in currants. Stir in ¾ cup of milk. Stir in additional milk, 1 tablespoon at a time, until dough leaves side of bowl and forms a ball.

3 Place dough on lightly floured surface; gently roll in flour to coat. Knead lightly 10 times. On ungreased cookie sheet, roll or pat dough into 9-inch round. Brush lightly with milk and sprinkle with 1 teaspoon sugar. Cut into 8 wedges with sharp knife or pizza cutter that has been dipped in flour, but do not separate wedges.

4 Bake 12 to 15 minutes or until light golden brown. Immediately remove from cookie sheet; carefully separate wedges. Serve warm with butter and/or honey.

1 Scone Calories 240; Total Fat 8g (Saturated Fat 5g, Trans Fat 0g); Cholesterol 20mg; Sodium 330mg; Total Carbohydrate 36g (Dietary Fiber 1g); Protein 4g **Carbohydrate Choices:** 2½

We found this recipe in our 1990 files. We love the attention to detail in the choice of ingredients—brown sugar and half-and-half give these scones an elevated richness, while sprinkling them with sugar before baking adds another layer of texture. These are a great make-ahead breakfast idea to cover the week or to serve at brunch.

Chocolate Chip Scones

Prep Time: 10 Minutes
Start to Finish: 25 Minutes
19 scones

4 cups Bisquick Original Pancake & Baking Mix
½ cup packed brown sugar
5 tablespoons butter, softened
¾ cup semisweet chocolate chips

½ cup half-and-half
2 eggs
Granulated sugar, if desired
Strawberry preserves, if desired

1 Heat oven to 450°F.

2 In large bowl, mix Bisquick mix and brown sugar. Cut in butter using pastry blender or fork until mixture looks like fine crumbs. Stir in chocolate chips, half-and-half, and eggs just until dry ingredients are moistened.

3 Place dough on surface lightly dusted with Bisquick mix. Roll dough to ½-inch thickness. With 2½-inch floured round cutter, cut into 19 rounds, rerolling dough scraps as necessary. Onto ungreased cookie sheet, place scones. Sprinkle with sugar.

4 Bake 10 to 12 minutes or until golden brown. Serve warm with preserves.

1 Scone Calories 210; Total Fat 10g (Saturated Fat 4.5g, Trans Fat 1g); Cholesterol 30mg; Sodium 350mg; Total Carbohydrate 27g (Dietary Fiber 1g); Protein 3g **Carbohydrate Choices:** 2

Over the years, several varieties of Bisquick have been produced. Today, Original, Gluten Free, and Heart Smart™ varieties are available.

Just begging for a fall or winter day, these glazed biscuits from our *Soups and Breads* magazine from the '90s pair the flavors of maple and pecan in a fantastic breakfast option.

Maple-Pecan Biscuits

Prep Time: 10 Minutes
Start to Finish: 25 Minutes
12 biscuits

BISCUITS
2 cups Gold Medal all-purpose flour
2 tablespoons granulated sugar
2 teaspoons baking powder
1 teaspoon salt
½ cup vegetable shortening
⅓ cup chopped pecans or walnuts
1 cup milk
2 teaspoons maple extract

GLAZE
½ cup powdered sugar
¼ teaspoon maple extract
2 to 3 teaspoons milk

1 Heat oven to 400°F. Grease large cookie sheet with vegetable shortening or spray with cooking spray.

2 In medium bowl, mix flour, granulated sugar, baking powder, and salt. Cut in shortening using pastry blender or fork until mixture looks like fine crumbs. Stir in pecans. In small bowl, mix milk and maple extract; stir into flour mixture just until flour is moistened. Drop dough by 12 spoonfuls onto cookie sheet.

3 Bake 10 to 12 minutes or until tops just begin to turn golden brown.

4 Immediately remove from cookie sheet to cooling rack (place rack on waxed paper to catch glaze drips). In small bowl, stir all glaze ingredients until smooth and thin enough to drizzle. Drizzle glaze over biscuits. Serve warm.

1 Biscuit Calories 220; Total Fat 11g (Saturated Fat 2.5g, Trans Fat 1.5g); Cholesterol 0mg; Sodium 290mg; Total Carbohydrate 25g (Dietary Fiber 1g); Protein 3g **Carbohydrate Choices:** 1½

We looked everywhere for the Bisquick pumpkin biscuit recipe Peter M. remembered so fondly. We got out the sunny yellow box and took a crack at re-creating the recipe for today. We're obsessed!

Bisquick Pumpkin Biscuits

Prep Time: 15 Minutes
Start to Finish: 30 Minutes
8 biscuits

3 tablespoons sugar
2 teaspoons pumpkin pie spice
2½ cups Bisquick Original Pancake & Baking Mix
2 tablespoons butter, softened

¾ cup canned pumpkin (from 15-oz can; not pumpkin pie mix)
¼ cup milk

1 Heat oven to 450°F.

2 In small bowl, mix 1 teaspoon of the sugar and ¼ teaspoon of the pumpkin pie spice; set aside.

3 In large bowl, mix remaining 2 tablespoons and 2 teaspoons sugar, the remaining 1¾ teaspoons pumpkin pie spice, and Bisquick mix. Cut in butter using pastry blender or fork until mixture looks like fine crumbs. Stir in pumpkin and milk just until soft dough forms.

4 Place dough on work surface sprinkled with Bisquick mix. Knead lightly 3 or 4 times. Roll or pat until ¾ inch thick. Cut with 2½-inch round cutter; reroll dough to cut out all biscuits. On ungreased cookie sheet, place dough rounds about 1 inch apart for crusty sides or touching for soft sides. Sprinkle tops with reserved pumpkin pie spice mixture.

5 Bake 10 to 12 minutes or until golden brown. Serve warm.

Cinnamon-Honey Butter: In small bowl, mix ½ cup softened butter, 2 tablespoons honey, and ¼ teaspoon ground cinnamon with spoon until light and fluffy.

Kitchen Notes: We started talking about what the perfect topping for these might be. We were practically drooling when we topped the warm biscuits with Cinnamon-Honey Butter (above) or plain, softened butter and jam.

1 Biscuit Calories 200; Total Fat 4.5g (Saturated Fat 2.5g, Trans Fat 0g); Cholesterol 10mg; Sodium 380mg; Total Carbohydrate 35g (Dietary Fiber 1g); Protein 3g **Carbohydrate Choices:** 2

From the Betty Crocker *Holiday* magazine (1994). This recipe is almost too pretty to eat . . . but we didn't let it get the best of us! Fluffy cake with chocolate chips and raspberries, topped with a delicious streusel . . . ooh, it's a winner.

Raspberry-Chocolate Coffee Cake

Prep Time: 15 Minutes
Start to Finish: 1 Hour
  5 Minutes
12 servings

STREUSEL
1/3 cup Gold Medal
  all-purpose flour
1/4 cup sugar

1/4 cup cold butter,
  cut into pieces
1/3 cup slivered almonds

COFFEE CAKE
2 cups Gold Medal
  all-purpose flour
3/4 cup sugar
1/4 cup butter, softened

1 cup milk
1 teaspoon vanilla
2 teaspoons baking powder
1/2 teaspoon salt
1 egg
1 cup semisweet chocolate chips
1 cup fresh or frozen
  raspberries

1 Heat oven to 350°F. Grease 9-inch square pan with vegetable shortening or spray with cooking spray.

2 In small bowl, mix 1/3 cup flour and 1/4 cup sugar. Cut in 1/4 cup butter with fork until crumbly. Stir in almonds; set streusel aside.

3 In large bowl, beat all coffee cake ingredients except chocolate chips and raspberries with electric mixer on low speed 30 seconds, scraping bowl constantly. Beat on medium speed 2 minutes, scraping bowl occasionally. Spread half of the batter in pan. Sprinkle with half each of the chocolate chips, raspberries, and streusel. Repeat with remaining batter, chocolate chips, raspberries, and streusel.

4 Bake about 50 minutes or until toothpick inserted in center comes out clean. Serve warm or cool. To serve, cut into 4 rows by 3 rows.

1 Serving Calories 340; Total Fat 15g (Saturated Fat 8g, Trans Fat 0g); Cholesterol 40mg; Sodium 260mg; Total Carbohydrate 47g (Dietary Fiber 2g); Protein 5g **Carbohydrate Choices:** 3

An example of how products change with the times. Our 1989 muffin mix came out during the oat bran craze of the late '80s.

People loved this recipe for the pillow-soft texture the rolls got from the added mashed potatoes. The dough can be made ahead of time, so you can bake piping-hot rolls whenever you want! We brought it back because it's just that good. Use it to make savory rolls (below), sweet Magic Cinnamon Balloon Buns (page 145), or Butterfly Rolls (page 146).

Refrigerator Roll Dough

Prep Time: 15 Minutes
Start to Finish: 10 Hours
　15 Minutes
48 rolls

1½ cups warm water
　(100°F to 110°F)
1 package regular active dry
　yeast (2¼ teaspoons)
1 cup lukewarm mashed
　potatoes
⅔ cup sugar

⅔ cup butter, softened
1 teaspoon salt
2 eggs
7 to 7½ cups Gold Medal
　all-purpose flour

1 In large bowl, place water. Stir in yeast until dissolved. Stir in potatoes, sugar, butter, salt, eggs, and 4 cups of the flour. Beat until smooth. Stir in enough remaining flour until dough pulls from sides of bowl.

2 Place dough on lightly floured surface. Knead 5 minutes or until smooth and elastic. Grease large bowl with vegetable shortening or spray with cooking spray. Place dough in bowl, turning to grease all sides. Cover bowl loosely with plastic wrap; refrigerate at least 8 hours or up to 5 days.

3 Punch dough to remove air bubbles. Divide dough into 4 equal parts. Shape dough parts into desired roll shape (recipes follow). Cover with plastic wrap; let rise in warm place about 1½ hours or until doubled in size.

4 Heat oven to 400°F.

5 Uncover and bake rolls 13 to 18 minutes or until golden brown.

Cloverleaf Rolls: Grease 12 regular-size muffin cups with shortening or spray with cooking spray. Prepare as directed through Step 3. Divide 1 part dough into 1-inch balls. Place 3 balls in each muffin cup. Cover and let rise as directed. Brush with 1 tablespoon melted butter. Bake as directed in Step 4. Makes 12 rolls.

Crescent Rolls: Grease large cookie sheet with vegetable shortening or spray with cooking spray. Prepare as directed through Step 3. Roll 1 part dough into 12-inch round about ¼ inch thick. Spread with 1 tablespoon softened butter. Cut into 12 wedges. Roll up starting at rounded edge. Arrange rolls point side down on cookie sheet. Curve slightly. Cover and let rise as directed. Brush with 1 tablespoon melted butter. Bake as directed in Step 4. Makes 12 rolls.

Fan Tan Rolls: Grease 12 regular-size muffin cups with vegetable shortening or spray with cooking spray. Prepare as directed through Step 3. On floured work surface, roll 1 part dough into 13×9-inch rectangle. Spread with 2 tablespoons softened butter. From short side, cut into 6 rows. Stack strips; cut crosswise into 12 stacks. Place cut side down in muffin cups. Cover and let rise as directed. Brush with 1 tablespoon melted butter. Bake as directed in Step 4. Makes 12 rolls.

Four-Leaf-Clover Rolls: Grease 12 regular-size muffin cups with vegetable shortening or spray with cooking spray. Prepare as directed through Step 3. Shape 1 part dough into 12 (2-inch) balls. Place 1 ball in each muffin cup. With scissors, snip each ball in half (not quite to the bottom) and then into quarters (not quite to the bottom). Cover and let rise as directed. Brush with 1 tablespoon melted butter. Bake as directed in Step 4. Makes 12 rolls.

Make-Ahead Directions: Wrap cooled rolls in aluminum foil; place in resealable freezer bag. Freeze up to 3 months. Just before serving, remove bag and heat rolls in foil in oven at 350°F about 20 minutes or until hot.

---

1 Roll Calories 110; Total Fat 3g (Saturated Fat 1.5g, Trans Fat 0g); Cholesterol 15mg; Sodium 75mg; Total Carbohydrate 18g (Dietary Fiber 0g); Protein 2g **Carbohydrate Choices:** 1

Appearing in the 1969 version of the *Betty Crocker Cookbook*, we wondered, are these pastries really magic? The marshmallow inside melts, leaving hollow centers with sweet, gooey filling you can sink your teeth into. They get a resounding yes!

Magic Cinnamon Balloon Buns

Prep Time: 15 Minutes
Start to Finish: 1 Hour
  40 Minutes
18 buns

2 parts Refrigerator Roll Dough
  (page 142)
1 cup sugar
1 tablespoon ground cinnamon

18 large marshmallows
½ cup butter, melted

1 Grease 18 regular-size muffin cups with vegetable shortening or spray with cooking spray. Place dough on generously floured work surface. Roll 2 dough parts together until dough is ⅛ inch thick. With 3½-inch floured round cutter, cut into 18 rounds.

2 In small bowl, mix sugar and cinnamon. For each bun, roll a marshmallow in melted butter, coating all sides; roll in cinnamon sugar. Wrap a dough round around the marshmallow, pinching edge together tightly at bottom.

Roll bun in butter and then in cinnamon sugar. Place seam side down in muffin cups. Repeat with remaining marshmallows, butter, cinnamon sugar, and dough rounds. Cover loosely with plastic wrap and let rise in warm place about 1 hour or until doubled in size.

3 Heat oven to 375°F.

4 Uncover and bake 20 to 25 minutes or until golden brown. Remove from pans to cooling rack. Serve warm.

1 Bun Calories 260; Total Fat 9g (Saturated Fat 6g, Trans Fat 0g); Cholesterol 35mg; Sodium 150mg; Total Carbohydrate 41g (Dietary Fiber 1g); Protein 3g **Carbohydrate Choices:** 3

These adorable little butterfly rolls are so fun to make, your kids just might want to be your sous-chef. Once they're baking, the amazing aroma from the oven will be just too good to resist.

Butterfly Rolls

Prep Time: 20 Minutes
Start to Finish: 1 Hour 15 Minutes
18 rolls

ROLLS

½ cup plus 2 tablespoons granulated sugar

2½ teaspoons ground cinnamon

2 parts Refrigerator Roll Dough (page 142)

2 to 3 tablespoons butter, softened

½ cup Gold Medal all-purpose flour

2 tablespoons cold butter

GLAZE

1 cup powdered sugar

1 tablespoon milk

½ teaspoon vanilla

1 Spray cookie sheet with cooking spray or line with cooking parchment paper. In small bowl, mix ½ cup of the granulated sugar with 1 teaspoon of the cinnamon; set aside.

2 On lightly floured work surface, roll dough parts together with rolling pin into 18×9-inch rectangle. Spread with softened butter to within ¼ inch of edges; sprinkle with cinnamon sugar mixture. Roll rectangle up tightly, beginning at long side. Pinch edge of dough into roll to seal. With fingers, shape roll until evenly round. With dental floss or serrated knife, cut roll into 18 (1-inch) slices. Place a clean dowel in center of each slice; press almost through dough to form butterfly shape. Arrange rolls slightly apart on cookie sheet, pressed sides up.

3 In small bowl, mix flour, the remaining 2 tablespoons granulated sugar, remaining 1½ teaspoons ground cinnamon, and 2 tablespoons cold butter with fork until crumbly; sprinkle over rolls. Cover rolls loosely with plastic wrap and let rise in warm place about 40 minutes or until doubled in size.

4 Heat oven to 375°F.

5 Uncover and bake about 12 minutes or until golden brown.

6 In small bowl, mix powdered sugar, milk, and vanilla until smooth.

7 Drizzle glaze over warm rolls.

Betty's Cooking Tip: Cut down on the cleanup by using parchment on the cookie sheet rather than greasing it. When the rolls are baked, place the cookie sheet (with the rolls) on a cooling rack. Drizzle the glaze over the rolls, and the parchment will catch all of the drips!

1 Roll Calories 240; Total Fat 7g (Saturated Fat 4g, Trans Fat 0g); Cholesterol 25mg; Sodium 120mg; Total Carbohydrate 40g (Dietary Fiber 1g); Protein 3g **Carbohydrate Choices:** 2½

From our *Gold Medal Century of Success* cookbook, casserole breads, such as this one, were a common side dish to serve with main dishes, soup, or chili. It was an easy way to have homemade yeast bread without the kneading. This one is a favorite for its south-of-the-border flavors that make it a natural to pair with your favorite chili or Mexican-inspired meals.

No-Knead Chile Pepper–Cheese Bread

Prep Time: 15 Minutes
Start to Finish: 2 Hours 20 Minutes
1 loaf (12 slices)

1 package regular active dry yeast (2¼ teaspoons)
½ cup warm water (100°F to 110°F)
½ cup lukewarm milk
⅔ cup butter, softened
2 eggs
1 teaspoon salt

2½ cups Gold Medal all-purpose flour
½ cup plus 1 teaspoon yellow cornmeal
1 cup shredded pepper Jack cheese (4 oz)
2 tablespoons drained chopped green chiles (from 4-oz can)

1 In large bowl, dissolve yeast in warm water. Add milk, butter, eggs, salt, and 1 cup of the flour. Beat with electric mixer on low speed, scraping bowl constantly, 30 seconds. Beat on medium speed, scraping bowl occasionally, 2 minutes. Stir in remaining flour, ½ cup of the cornmeal, the cheese, and chiles. Scrape batter from side of bowl. Cover with plastic wrap and let rise in warm place about 30 minutes or until doubled in size.

2 Grease 2-quart round casserole with vegetable shortening or spray with cooking spray. Beat dough with wooden spoon 25 strokes to deflate; pour and spread evenly in casserole. Cover with plastic wrap and let rise in warm place about 40 minutes or until doubled in size.

3 Meanwhile, heat oven to 375°F.

4 Uncover loaf and sprinkle with remaining 1 teaspoon cornmeal. Bake 40 to 45 minutes or until loaf is golden brown and sounds hollow when tapped. Remove from casserole, cool on cooling rack. To serve, cut into 12 slices or 8 wedges with serrated knife. Serve warm or cool.

1 Slice Calories 270; Total Fat 15g (Saturated Fat 9g, Trans Fat 0.5g); Cholesterol 70mg; Sodium 280mg; Total Carbohydrate 27g (Dietary Fiber 1g); Protein 7g **Carbohydrate Choices:** 2

From Betty Crocker's *New Soup, Stew & Chili* magazine, these thin, cheese-topped breadsticks are as fun to make as they are to eat.

Cheesy Breadsticks

Prep Time: 45 Minutes
Start to Finish: 45 Minutes
24 breadsticks

2 cups Gold Medal all-purpose flour
½ cup shredded cheddar cheese (2 oz)
¾ cup milk
2 tablespoons butter, melted
2 teaspoons baking powder

1 teaspoon sugar
1 teaspoon salt
¼ cup grated Parmesan cheese
½ teaspoon paprika
1 egg, beaten

1 In large bowl, mix flour, cheddar cheese, milk, melted butter, baking powder, sugar, and salt until dough leaves side of bowl. Turn dough onto lightly floured surface; knead lightly 25 times. Cover and let stand 15 minutes.

2 Heat oven to 400°F. Grease 2 cookie sheets with vegetable shortening or spray with cooking spray.

3 In small bowl, mix Parmesan cheese and paprika; set aside. Divide dough in half. Cover one half; set aside. On lightly floured work surface, roll other in 10×8-inch rectangle. Brush with beaten egg; sprinkle with half of Parmesan mixture and press into dough. Cut rectangle lengthwise into 12 strips. Twist each strip several times; place on cookie sheet. Repeat with remaining dough, egg, and Parmesan mixture.

4 Bake 1 cookie sheet 12 to 15 minutes or until golden brown. Immediately remove breadsticks from cookie sheet to cooling rack. Repeat with second cookie sheet.

1 Breadstick Calories 70; Total Fat 2.5g (Saturated Fat 1.5g, Trans Fat 0g); Cholesterol 15mg; Sodium 180mg; Total Carbohydrate 9g (Dietary Fiber 0g); Protein 2g **Carbohydrate Choices:** ½

1959 Betty Crocker Quick Bread Sticks ad with directions how to make the product into several new recipes.

Entirely new discovery from
Betty Crocker's kitchen

Quick Bread Sticks!

Refrigerated and ready-to-bake

Some like 'em crusty! Here's the baking surprise of your life. Lively dough with sesame seeds, marked off in sticks, ready to bake *as you choose.* For the long thin bread sticks, crusty outside and tender inside, roll each strip of dough with your hands. Bake, and get 10 bread sticks to serve with salad, chili, spaghetti, steak!

Some like 'em soft! For soft-sided finger-size "rolls" you'll bake the lively dough just as it comes from the container, without separating. Minutes later, hot "rolls" for any meal at all! Complete directions for both kinds are on the package. Get *two,* make bread sticks *both* ways, and see which the family likes best.

"Goodness! Imagine serving really fresh-baked bread sticks or finger 'rolls' this easily. And as we developed these in our kitchens, we found many more delightful ways to use them; some of our new ideas are in the column at your right. Enjoy them!"

Betty Crocker

General Mills

In your grocer's dairy case

The original recipe for beer bread was made with only two ingredients—self-rising flour and beer. But since most people have all-purpose flour on hand, we've included this version that's just a few more ingredients. This hearty and flavorful no-knead bread is perfect to serve with a selection of sliced meats and cheeses, as an appetizer, or as part of a game day board for grazing.

Beer Bread

Prep Time: 10 Minutes
Start to Finish: 3 Hours
   10 Minutes
1 loaf (16 slices)

3 cups Gold Medal
   all-purpose flour
¼ cup sugar
3 teaspoons baking powder
1 teaspoon salt

1 bottle or can (12 oz) beer,
   room temperature
2 tablespoons butter, melted
Additional melted butter,
   if desired

1 Heat oven to 375°F. Grease 8×4-inch or 9×5-inch loaf pan with vegetable shortening or spray with cooking spray.

2 In large bowl, mix flour, sugar, baking powder, and salt. Stir in beer and 2 tablespoons melted butter just until moistened (batter will be lumpy). Spread in pan.

3 Bake 40 to 50 minutes or until toothpick inserted in center comes out clean and top is light golden. Brush top of loaf with additional butter. Cool 10 minutes in pan. Loosen sides of loaf from pan; remove from pan to wire rack. Cool completely, about 2 hours.

Garlic-Chive Beer Bread: After stirring in the beer and butter in Step 2, stir in 2 tablespoons chopped fresh chives and 2 cloves finely chopped garlic.

1 Slice Calories 110; Total Fat 1.5g (Saturated Fat 1g, Trans Fat 0g); Cholesterol 0mg; Sodium 240mg; Total Carbohydrate 21g (Dietary Fiber 0g); Protein 2g **Carbohydrate Choices:** 1½

Steaming-hot soup or stew served in bread bowls is the ultimate comfort food! We've brought back this yummy recipe that's as comfy as a big, snuggly sweater. Simply place the bread bowls on serving plates and fill with your favorite soup or stew, and then break off pieces of bread as you eat the soup. Delicious!

Parmesan Bread Bowls

Prep Time: 20 Minutes
Start to Finish: 1 Hour 25 Minutes
6 bowls

¼ cup warm water (105°F to 110°F)

1 package fast-acting dry yeast (2¼ teaspoons)

2 tablespoons sugar

3 cups Gold Medal all-purpose flour

⅓ cup grated Parmesan cheese

3 teaspoons baking powder

½ teaspoon salt

¼ cup butter

About 1 cup buttermilk

1 In small bowl, place warm water. Stir in yeast until dissolved. Stir in sugar; set aside. In large bowl, mix flour, Parmesan cheese, baking powder, and salt. Cut in butter using pastry blender or fork until mixture looks like fine crumbs. Stir in yeast mixture and just enough buttermilk so dough leaves side of bowl and forms a ball. On lightly floured surface, knead dough about 1 minute or until smooth. Cover and let rise in warm place 10 minutes.

2 Heat oven to 375°F. Grease outsides of 6 (10-oz) custard cups with vegetable shortening or spray with cooking spray. Place 3 cups, upside down, in ungreased 15×10×1-inch pan.

3 Divide dough into 6 equal parts. Pat or roll 3 of the parts into 7-inch rounds. Drape dough rounds over outsides of custard cups; do not allow dough to curl under edges of cups. Bake 3 bread bowls at a time; pat or roll dough for remaining bread bowls while first 3 bowls are baking.

4 Bake 18 to 22 minutes or until golden brown. Carefully lift bread bowls from custard cups (custard cups and bread will be hot). Cool bread bowls upright on cooling rack 10 minutes.

1 Bowl Calories 360; Total Fat 11g (Saturated Fat 6g, Trans Fat 0g); Cholesterol 30mg; Sodium 650mg; Total Carbohydrate 56g (Dietary Fiber 2g); Protein 10g **Carbohydrate Choices:** 4

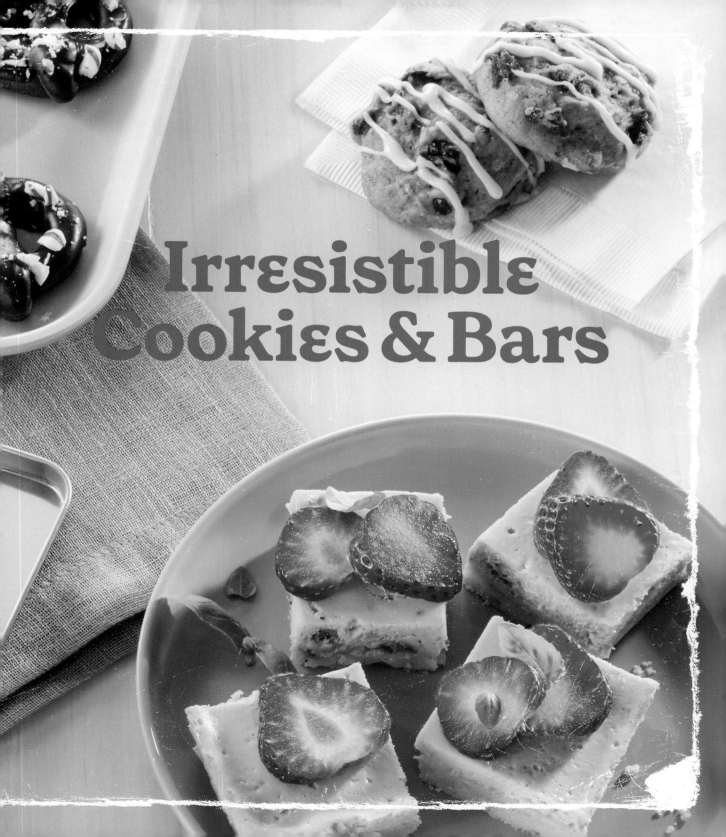

Irresistible
Cookies & Bars

What is a crinkle cookie? Usually, the dough is shaped into balls and rolled in sugar. When they are baked, they form small cracks on the tops, giving them their welcoming name. We love this flavor combo from *Betty Crocker's Old-Fashioned Desserts* cookbook (1992).

Lemon-Ginger Crinkles

Prep Time: 15 Minutes
Start to Finish: 1 Hour
5 Minutes
About 4 dozen cookies

1 cup packed brown sugar
½ cup vegetable shortening
1 tablespoon lemon zest
1 egg
1½ cups Gold Medal
all-purpose flour

½ teaspoon baking soda
½ teaspoon cream of tartar
¼ teaspoon salt
¼ teaspoon ground ginger
Granulated sugar

1 Heat oven to 350°F.

2 In large bowl, mix brown sugar, shortening, lemon zest, and egg until well blended. Stir in remaining ingredients except granulated sugar.

3 In small bowl, place granulated sugar. Shape dough into 1-inch balls; dip tops into granulated sugar. Onto each of 2 ungreased cookie sheets, arrange balls, sugared sides up, about 3 inches apart.

4 Bake 1 cookie sheet 10 to 11 minutes or until almost no indentation remains when touched. Immediately remove from cookie sheet to cooling rack. Repeat with second cookie sheet.

5 Onto completely cooled cookie sheets, continue forming and baking cookies as directed in Steps 3 and 4.

How to Store: Store these cookies in a tightly covered container at room temperature.

1 Cookie Calories 50; Total Fat 2.5g (Saturated Fat 0.5g, Trans Fat 0g); Cholesterol 0mg; Sodium 30mg; Total Carbohydrate 8g (Dietary Fiber 0g); Protein 0g **Carbohydrate Choices:** ½

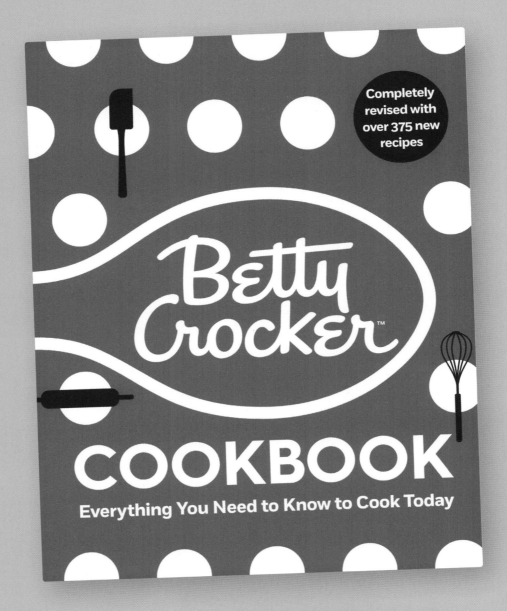

Completely revised with over 375 new recipes

Betty Crocker™

COOKBOOK

Everything You Need to Know to Cook Today

The *Betty Crocker Cookbook* (currently in its 13th edition) is frequently requested and often given as a shower or wedding gift, or when a kid goes off to college or gets their first apartment, since it is a one-stop resource for stocking a pantry, how to entertain, food storage and cooking charts, plus oodles of recipes, both classic favorites and on-trend new favorites.

We can see why Fern remembers these cookies fondly—they are moist, chewy, and have the taste of the tropics. These little jewels appeared in the 1956 version of *Betty Crocker's Picture Cook Book*.

Pineapple Cookies

Prep Time: 20 Minutes
Start to Finish: 2 Hours 10 Minutes
About 5 dozen cookies

1 cup shortening
1½ cups sugar
1 egg
1 cup crushed pineapple with juice (from 20-oz can)

3½ cups Gold Medal all-purpose flour
1 teaspoon baking soda
¼ teaspoon ground nutmeg
½ cup chopped nuts

1 In large bowl, mix shortening, sugar, and egg until well blended. Stir in pineapple with juice. Stir in remaining ingredients except nuts. Stir in nuts. Cover and refrigerate at least 1 hour.

2 Heat oven to 400°F. Lightly grease 2 cookie sheets with vegetable shortening or spray with cooking spray.

3 Drop dough by rounded teaspoonfuls about 2 inches apart.

4 Bake 1 cookie sheet 8 to 10 minutes or until no imprint remains when touched lightly. Immediately remove cookies from cookie sheet to cooling rack. Repeat with second cookie sheet.

5 Onto completely cooled cookie sheets, continue forming and baking cookies as directed in Steps 3 and 4.

How to Store: Store these cookies at room temperature in resealable food-storage plastic bags or tightly covered containers.

1 Cookie Calories 90; Total Fat 4g (Saturated Fat 1g, Trans Fat 0g); Cholesterol 0mg; Sodium 20mg; Total Carbohydrate 11g (Dietary Fiber 0g); Protein 1g **Carbohydrate Choices:** 1

Fan Memory

"My mother loved them and now my husband [does too, but we] lost the recipe."

—Fern K.

Kim B. told us she lost her family's recipe for Lemon-Hazelnut Cookies. In doing some recipe research to re-create the recipe for her, we found these cookies had a unique structure. Rather than being a flour-based dough, these cookies tended to be mostly egg whites and ground hazelnuts. The result? We were as delighted with the taste as we were with the texture. What a find!

Lemon-Hazelnut Cookies

Prep Time: 25 Minutes
Start to Finish: 1 Hour
15 Minutes
About 2 dozen cookies

2 cups hazelnuts
2 egg whites
2 teaspoons lemon zest
4 teaspoons fresh lemon juice
½ cup granulated sugar

¼ teaspoon salt
½ cup powdered sugar
Additional chopped hazelnuts, if desired

1 Heat oven to 350°F. Spread 2 cups hazelnuts in ungreased shallow pan. Bake uncovered 8 to 10 minutes, stirring occasionally, until skins begin to crack and flake. Transfer hazelnuts to clean kitchen towel; rub with towel vigorously to remove skins. Cool slightly.

2 In food processor, place nuts. Cover and process until coarsely ground.

3 Line 2 cookie sheets with cooking parchment paper.

4 In medium bowl, beat egg whites with whisk until foamy. Gently stir in hazelnuts, lemon zest, 2 teaspoons of the lemon juice, the granulated sugar, and salt (mixture may be slightly sticky). Onto each cookie sheet drop rounded teaspoonfuls of dough about 1 inch apart.

5 Bake 1 cookie sheet 11 to 12 minutes or until cookies are set and light brown. Cool 2 minutes; remove from cookie sheet to wire rack. Repeat with remaining cookie sheet. Cool cookies completely, about 15 minutes.

6 In small bowl, stir together powdered sugar and remaining 2 teaspoons lemon juice until smooth. Drizzle cookies with icing. Sprinkle with additional chopped hazelnuts.

Kitchen Notes: We found it essential to be sure you have 2 cups of nuts for the ingredient proportions to be correct and get the full yield of cookies. Our testing found that while small packages of nuts would indicate how many cups it contained, it didn't necessarily measure that way. If purchasing packages that say they contain 2 cups or less, you might want to purchase one extra for this reason.

How to Store: Store at room temperature in a tightly covered container.

1 Cookie Calories 90; Total Fat 6g (Saturated Fat 0g, Trans Fat 0g); Cholesterol 0mg; Sodium 30mg; Total Carbohydrate 8g (Dietary Fiber 1g); Protein 1g **Carbohydrate Choices:** ½

These sweetly spiced pumpkin cookies are perfect when you have a yearning for a pumpkin treat. From our 1996 *Betty Crocker Cookbook*, they originally called for dates, but you could substitute chopped dried cherries, raisins, or dried cranberries just as easily. Use whatever you have on hand or make them with a different fruit each time, as a fun surprise.

Spiced Pumpkin-Date Cookies

Prep Time: 15 Minutes
Start to Finish: 1 Hour
About 4 dozen cookies

1 cup sugar
½ cup butter, softened

1 cup canned pumpkin
  (not pumpkin pie mix)
2 eggs
2 cups Gold Medal
  all-purpose flour
2 teaspoons baking powder
2 teaspoons ground cinnamon

½ teaspoon ground nutmeg
½ teaspoon ground ginger
¼ teaspoon ground cloves
1 cup chopped dates or
  dried cherries, raisins, or
  sweetened dried cranberries
½ cup chopped nuts, if desired

1 Heat oven to 375°F.

2 In large bowl, beat sugar and butter with electric mixer on medium speed until light and fluffy, or mix with spoon. Beat in pumpkin and eggs. Stir in remaining ingredients except dates and nuts. Stir in dates and nuts. Onto each of 2 ungreased cookie sheets, drop dough by rounded teaspoonfuls about 2 inches apart. Flatten slightly, if desired.

3 Bake 1 cookie sheet 8 to 10 minutes or until edges are set. Immediately remove from cookie sheet to cooling rack. Repeat with second cookie sheet.

4 Onto completely cooled cookie sheets, continue forming and baking cookies as directed in Steps 2 and 3.

Glazed Spiced Pumpkin-Date Cookies: Prepare the glaze portion of Almond-Filled Crescents (page 38) and drizzle over.

Betty's Cooking Tip: Add the goodness of oats, if you like, by substituting ½ cup old-fashioned oats for ½ cup of the flour.

How to Store: Store at room temperature in resealable food-storage plastic bags or tightly covered containers.

1 Cookie Calories 70; Total Fat 2g (Saturated Fat 1.5g, Trans Fat 0g); Cholesterol 15mg; Sodium 40mg; Total Carbohydrate 11g (Dietary Fiber 0g); Protein 1g **Carbohydrate Choices:** 1

Refreshment Time!
New ideas from Betty Crocker

"Desserts—for 'C'mon over for dessert' time. Snacks—for neighborly TV watching. That little 'something extra' to share at coffee time. Our Betty Crocker Cake Mixes were born to make refreshments easy, to make entertaining something you'll want to do often. Bake one up, why don't you, for refreshments . . . and the family . . . today!

"I guarantee a perfect* cake— homemade-perfect—*cake . . . after cake . . . after cake*"!

Betty Crocker   (General Mills)

Second breakfast — Hot Buttered Cake! Use 1 extra egg yolk in Betty Crocker Honey Spice Cake Mix batter. Bake in two 8½x4½x2¾" loaf pans 35 to 45 min. at 350°. Serve hot with butter and jelly. Mmm!

Afternoon coffee break—Upside-Downies! Follow cupcake directions on Yellow Cake Mix pkg. Place ½ tsp. butter, 1 tsp. brown sugar (packed), and 1 peach half in each of 14 custard cups before adding batter.

Teatime treat — Loaf Cake Sandwiches! Use Betty Crocker Marble Cake. Bake batter in two 8½x4½x2¾" loaf pans 35 to 40 min. at 350°. Put slices together with Betty Crocker Chocolate Fudge Frosting Mix. Cut in party shapes.

*PERFECT! Yes, every mix we make for you is guaranteed to come out perfect, or send the box top to Betty Crocker, Box 200, Minneapolis, Minn., and General Mills will send your money back.

A 1958 Betty Crocker cake mix advertisement.

Love sweet and salty? Then these are the cookies for you. From our 1979 *Gold Medal Century of Success Cookbook*, the rich flavor of these cookies will be hard to resist.

Salted Peanut Crisps

Prep Time: 50 Minutes
Start to Finish: 1 Hour
  50 Minutes
About 6 dozen cookies

1½ cups packed brown sugar
½ cup butter, softened
½ cup vegetable shortening
2 teaspoons vanilla
2 eggs

3 cups Gold Medal
  all-purpose flour
½ teaspoon salt
½ teaspoon baking soda
2 cups salted cocktail peanuts
Granulated sugar

1 Heat oven to 375°F. Lightly grease 2 cookie sheets with shortening or spray with cooking spray.

2 In large bowl, mix brown sugar, butter, shortening, vanilla, and eggs until well blended. Stir in remaining ingredients except peanuts and granulated sugar. Stir in peanuts.

3 Shape dough by rounded teaspoonfuls into balls. Onto each cookie sheet, arrange 12 balls about 2 inches apart. Flatten with bottom of glass dipped in granulated sugar.

4 Bake 1 cookie sheet 8 to 10 minutes or until golden brown. Immediately remove from cookie sheet to cooling rack. Repeat with second cookie sheet.

5 Onto completely cooled cookie sheets, continue forming and baking cookies as directed in Steps 3 and 4.

Betty's Cooking Tip: Cocktail peanuts are typically found in cans near the other nuts at the grocery store. They are oilier than dry-roasted peanuts, giving them a terrific texture for these cookies.

How to Store: Store these cookies at room temperature in loosely covered containers.

1 Cookie Calories 90; Total Fat 5g (Saturated Fat 1.5g, Trans Fat 0g); Cholesterol 10mg; Sodium 55mg; Total Carbohydrate 9g (Dietary Fiber 0g); Protein 1g **Carbohydrate Choices:** ½

Don't let the simple ingredients of these cookies fool you. From our 1969 *Betty Crocker Cookbook*, these easy-to-prepare cookies are loaded with homemade flavor.

Vanilla Crispies

Prep Time: 20 Minutes
Start to Finish: 2 Hours
About 6 dozen cookies

1 cup sugar
1 cup butter, softened
2 cups Gold Medal all-purpose or whole wheat flour
2 teaspoons vanilla

½ teaspoon baking soda
½ teaspoon cream of tartar
1 egg
Additional sugar, for dipping

1 In large bowl, mix 1 cup sugar and the butter until well blended. Stir in remaining ingredients except extra sugar for dipping. Cover and refrigerate 1 hour.

2 Heat oven to 375°F.

3 Shape level tablespoonfuls of dough into 1-inch balls. Onto each of 2 ungreased cookie sheets, arrange 12 balls about 2 inches apart. Flatten with bottom of glass dipped in sugar.

4 Bake 1 cookie sheet 8 to 10 minutes or until light brown. Immediately remove from cookie sheet to cooling rack. Repeat with second cookie sheet.

5 Onto completely cooled cookie sheets, continue forming and baking cookies as directed in Steps 3 and 4.

Brown Sugar Crispies: Substitute ½ cup packed brown sugar for ½ cup of the granulated sugar.

How to Store: Store these cookies at room temperature in loosely covered containers.

1 Cookie Calories 50; Total Fat 2.5g (Saturated Fat 1.5g, Trans Fat 0g); Cholesterol 10mg; Sodium 10mg; Total Carbohydrate 5g (Dietary Fiber 0g); Protein 0g **Carbohydrate Choices:** ½

From our 1979 *Century of Success Cookbook*, these colorful, citrusy refrigerator cookies really stand out from the crowd.

Fruit-Slice Cookies

Prep Time: 40 Minutes
Start to Finish: 5 Hours
   20 Minutes
About 5 dozen cookies

COOKIES
½ cup granulated sugar
½ cup butter, softened
¾ teaspoon vanilla
1 egg
1½ cups Gold Medal
   all-purpose flour
½ teaspoon salt
Yellow, green, and orange
   liquid or gel food colors
¾ teaspoon lemon zest
¾ teaspoon lime zest
¾ teaspoon orange zest
Yellow, green, and orange
   sugars, if desired

DECORATOR'S FROSTING
2 cups powdered sugar
2 tablespoons water or milk
½ teaspoon vanilla

1 In medium bowl, mix granulated sugar, butter, vanilla, and egg until well blended. Stir in flour and salt. Divide dough into 4 equal parts; place 3 parts in separate small bowls (leave remaining part on work surface). Into 1 part, mix a few drops yellow food color and lemon zest with hands until evenly colored. Repeat with another part, using green food color and lime zest. Repeat with third part, using orange food color and orange zest. Leave fourth part on work surface plain.

2 Shape each colored part by rolling between hands into a log about 2 inches in diameter. Divide plain dough into 3 equal parts. On work surface dusted lightly with flour, roll each part into rectangle 3×4 inches. Wrap a rectangle around each colored log; press together. Roll in matching colored sugar. Wrap and refrigerate rolls at least 4 hours.

3 Heat oven to 400°F.

4 With sharp knife, from each roll, cut into about ⅛-inch slices; cut each slice crosswise in half. Onto each of 2 ungreased cookie sheets, arrange 12 cookies about 1 inch apart.

5 Bake 1 cookie sheet 6 to 8 minutes or until cookies are set. Immediately remove from cookie sheet to cooling rack. Repeat with second cookie sheet.

6 Onto completely cooled cookie sheets, continue slicing and baking cookies as directed in Steps 4 and 5.

7 In medium bowl, mix frosting ingredients with spoon until smooth and spreadable. Using decorator bag fitted with small decorating tip or quart-size resealable bag, fill bag with frosting. (Cut tiny corner from bag if using a resealable bag.) Pipe frosting onto cookies.

{ recipe continues }

Betty's Cooking Tip: For a nice, round log, roll it over just occasionally during the refrigeration step, to keep it from forming a flattened side.

Betty's Cooking Tip: Line the cooled dirty cookie sheets with parchment paper before frosting the cooled cookies to cut down on the cleanup.

How to Store: Let the frosting on these cookies set or harden before storing; store by placing cookies between layers of parchment or waxed paper, plastic wrap, or foil. Store at room temperature in resealable food-storage plastic bags or tightly covered containers.

1 Cookie Calories 50; Total Fat 1.5g (Saturated Fat 1g, Trans Fat 0g); Cholesterol 5mg; Sodium 35mg; Total Carbohydrate 8g (Dietary Fiber 0g); Protein 0g **Carbohydrate Choices:** ½

1950 Betty Crocker newsletter with menu, recipes, and entertaining tips.

Refrigerator cookies or "icebox cookies" were popular in the 1930s, with the idea being that you could make fresh, warm cookies at a moment's notice. We love this recipe for its vintage combination of oats with molasses, lemon, and vanilla flavors. No wonder we've had requests to find it again!

Oatmeal Refrigerator Cookies

Prep Time: 20 Minutes
Start to Finish: 4 Hours 5 Minutes
About 5 dozen cookies

½ cup granulated sugar
½ cup packed brown sugar
½ cup butter, softened
2 tablespoons molasses
1½ teaspoons lemon zest
½ teaspoon vanilla
1 egg

1½ cups Gold Medal all-purpose flour
1½ cups quick-cooking or old-fashioned oats
½ teaspoon baking soda
¼ teaspoon salt

1 In large bowl, mix granulated sugar, brown sugar, butter, molasses, lemon zest, vanilla, and egg until well blended. Stir in remaining ingredients (dough will be stiff). Shape into a 15-inch-long log. Wrap with plastic wrap and refrigerate at least 3 hours.

2 Heat oven to 375°F.

3 Unwrap and cut into ¼-inch-thick slices. Onto each of 2 ungreased cookie sheets, arrange slices 2 inches apart.

4 Bake 1 cookie sheet 7 to 9 minutes or until edges begin to brown. Cool 1 to 2 minutes; remove cookies from cookie sheet to cooling rack. Repeat with second cookie sheet.

5 Onto completely cooled cookie sheets, continue slicing and baking cookies as directed in Steps 3 and 4.

How to Store: The dough may be stored tightly wrapped in refrigerator and sliced and baked as you'd like them. Keep dough for no longer than 1 week in refrigerator. Or to freeze, place wrapped cookie dough log in freezer until firm. Once dough is firm, make sure ends of plastic are twisted, and place log in large resealable freezer bag. Freeze up to 1 month. To thaw, let dough stand 30 to 45 minutes at room temperature or until easy to cut into slices. Remove plastic, slice, and continue as directed in recipe. Store baked cookies in a tightly covered container at room temperature for up to 5 days.

1 Cookie Calories 50; Total Fat 2g (Saturated Fat 1g, Trans Fat 0g); Cholesterol 5mg; Sodium 35mg; Total Carbohydrate 8g (Dietary Fiber 0g); Protein 0g **Carbohydrate Choices:** ½

From *Betty Crocker's Old-Fashioned Desserts*, this recipe was made true to its roots, with black walnuts, because they grew in the wild in the United States and were part of many Native American diets. They have a rich, bold, distinctive flavor. Today, you may find them in larger grocery or big-box stores or online. Most of the walnuts we use today are English walnuts. They have a milder flavor than the black variety. Use whichever kind you like in these rich, buttery cookies.

Butterscotch-Walnut Sugar Cookies

Prep Time: 45 Minutes
Start to Finish: 2 Hours
About 4 dozen cookies

1 cup packed brown sugar
½ cup butter, softened
¼ cup vegetable shortening
1 teaspoon vanilla
2 eggs
2½ cups Gold Medal all-purpose flour

1 teaspoon baking powder
¾ teaspoon salt
1 cup finely chopped black or regular walnuts
Coarse sugar, if desired

1 In large bowl, beat brown sugar, butter, shortening, vanilla, and eggs with electric mixer on medium speed until well blended. Stir in flour, baking powder, and salt. Stir in walnuts. Divide dough in half; shape each half into disk. Wrap in plastic wrap. Refrigerate at least 1 hour.

2 Heat oven to 400°F.

3 Roll one dough disk on lightly floured surface until ⅛ inch thick. Cut with 3-inch cookie cutters. Reroll scraps to cut additional cookies. Onto each of 2 ungreased cookie sheets, arrange cutouts about 1 inch apart. Sprinkle with coarse sugar.

4 Bake 1 cookie sheet 5 to 7 minutes or until edges are light brown. Immediately remove cookies from cookie sheet to cooling rack. Repeat with second cookie sheet.

5 Onto completely cooled cookie sheets, continue cutting out and baking cookies as directed in Steps 3 and 4.

How to Store: Store these cookies loosely covered at room temperature.

1 Cookie Calories 70; Total Fat 3.5g (Saturated Fat 1.5g, Trans Fat 0g); Cholesterol 15mg; Sodium 65mg; Total Carbohydrate 10g (Dietary Fiber 0g); Protein 1g **Carbohydrate Choices:** ½

The spices in these cookies were a popular combination used in baked goods of the 1900s. The old-fashioned flavor of these cookies, spread with a creamy frosting for just the right amount of sweetness, is like a sweet, magical trip back to simpler times.

Ginger Creams

Prep Time: 25 Minutes
Start to Finish: 2 Hours
About 3 dozen cookies

COOKIES
½ cup granulated sugar

⅓ cup vegetable shortening or butter, softened

½ cup mild-flavor (light) or full-flavor (dark) molasses

½ cup water

1 egg

2 cups Gold Medal all-purpose flour

1 teaspoon ground ginger

½ teaspoon salt

½ teaspoon baking soda

½ teaspoon ground nutmeg

½ teaspoon ground cloves

½ teaspoon ground cinnamon

FROSTING
3 cups powdered sugar

⅓ cup butter, softened

1 to 2 tablespoons milk

1½ teaspoons vanilla

1 In large bowl, beat granulated sugar, shortening, molasses, water, and egg with electric mixer on medium speed until well blended. Stir in remaining cookie ingredients. Cover and refrigerate at least 1 hour.

2 Heat oven to 400°F. Line 2 cookie sheets with cooking parchment paper.

3 Onto cookie sheets, drop dough by rounded tablespoonfuls about 2 inches apart.

4 Bake 1 cookie sheet 7 to 9 minutes or until almost no indentation remains when touched. Cool 1 minute; remove from cookie sheet to cooling rack. Repeat with second cookie sheet.

5 Onto completely cooled cookie sheets, continue forming and baking cookies as directed in Steps 3 and 4.

6 In large bowl, mix powdered sugar and butter with spoon or electric mixer on low speed until blended. Beat in 1 tablespoon of the milk and the vanilla. Gradually beat in just enough remaining milk, 1 teaspoon at a time, to make frosting smooth and spreadable. Frost tops of cookies.

Betty's Cooking Tip: For a little something extra, mix a little additional ground nutmeg and ginger and sprinkle it lightly over the frosted cookies.

How to Store: Store in tightly covered container with cooking parchment or waxed paper between layers at room temperature.

1 Cookie Calories 130; Total Fat 4g (Saturated Fat 1.5g, Trans Fat 0g); Cholesterol 10mg; Sodium 55mg; Total Carbohydrate 22g (Dietary Fiber 0g); Protein 1g **Carbohydrate Choices:** 1½

If you're unfamiliar with cardamom, it has a spicy-sweet flavor that's widely used in Scandinavian and South Asian cooking. We love the aromatic flavor it brings to these cookies, mixed with cinnamon and almond.

Cardamom Cookies

Prep Time: 20 Minutes
Start to Finish: 1 Hour 10 Minutes
About 3½ dozen cookies

½ cup sugar
½ cup vegetable shortening
1 whole egg
1⅔ cups Gold Medal all-purpose flour
½ cup chopped slivered almonds, toasted*

1 teaspoon ground cardamom
1 teaspoon ground cinnamon
½ teaspoon baking powder
1 egg yolk
1 tablespoon water
About 42 blanched whole almonds

1 Heat oven to 375°F.

2 In medium bowl, mix sugar, shortening, and whole egg. Stir in flour, chopped almonds, cardamom, cinnamon, and baking powder.

3 Shape dough into 1-inch balls. Onto each of 2 ungreased cookie sheets, arrange 12 balls about 2 inches apart; flatten slightly with fingers. In small bowl, mix egg yolk and water; brush over cookies. Top each with whole almond.

4 Bake 1 cookie sheet 10 to 12 minutes or until golden brown. Immediately remove from cookie sheet to cooling rack. Repeat with second cookie sheet.

5 Onto completely cooled cookie sheets, continue forming and baking cookies as directed in Steps 3 and 4.

* To toast almonds: Heat oven to 350°F. Spread almonds in ungreased shallow pan. Bake uncovered 6 to 10 minutes, stirring occasionally, until light brown.

How to Store: Store these cookies at room temperature in resealable food-storage plastic bags or tightly covered containers.

1 Cookie Calories 70; Total Fat 4g (Saturated Fat 1g, Trans Fat 0g); Cholesterol 10mg; Sodium 10mg; Total Carbohydrate 7g (Dietary Fiber 0g); Protein 1g **Carbohydrate Choices:** ½

Pinwheels are a classic cookie shape that frequently found themselves in cookie jars or on cookie tray displays. We wanted to bring back this beloved date version as dates are enjoying a resurgence due in part to the fruit's reputation as a healthier option to refined sugar when sweetening dishes.

Date Pinwheels

Prep Time: 40 Minutes
Start to Finish: 5 Hours
30 Minutes
About 5 dozen cookies

12 oz chopped pitted dates
(from two 8-oz boxes)
1/3 cup granulated sugar
1/3 cup water
1 cup packed brown sugar
1/4 cup vegetable shortening

1/4 cup butter, softened
1/2 teaspoon vanilla
1 egg
1 3/4 cups Gold Medal
all-purpose flour
1/4 teaspoon salt

1 In 1-quart saucepan, cook dates, granulated sugar, and water over medium heat 4 to 7 minutes, stirring constantly, or until thickened. Cool completely.

2 In medium bowl, stir brown sugar, shortening, butter, vanilla, and egg with spoon until smooth. Stir in flour and salt. Divide dough in half. Cover work surface with waxed paper. Working with one dough half at a time, roll dough on waxed paper into an 11×7-inch rectangle. Spread half of date mixture over rectangle to within 1/4 inch of edges. Roll up beginning on long side. Pinch edge of dough into roll to seal. Repeat with remaining dough half and date filling. Wrap and refrigerate rolls at least 4 hours.

3 Heat oven to 400°F.

4 Cut twenty-four 1/4-inch slices from 1 roll. Onto each of 2 ungreased cookie sheets, arrange 12 slices about 1 inch apart.

5 Bake 1 cookie sheet about 10 minutes or until light brown. Immediately remove from cookie sheet to cooling rack. Repeat with second cookie sheet.

6 Onto completely cooled cookie sheets, continue slicing and baking cookies as directed in Steps 4 and 5.

How to Store: Store these cookies at room temperature in resealable food-storage plastic bags or tightly covered containers.

1 Cookie Calories 70; Total Fat 2g (Saturated Fat 0.5g, Trans Fat 0g); Cholesterol 5mg; Sodium 10mg; Total Carbohydrate 12g (Dietary Fiber 0g); Protein 0g **Carbohydrate Choices:** 1

From our 1979 *Century of Success Cookbook*, these delightful pretzel-shaped cookies are as much fun to make as they are to eat. It's like making an irresistibly delicious edible craft! Have your friends over for a pretzel-making party or engage the kids in this kitchen fun.

Chocolate Peppermint Cookie Twists

Prep Time: 1 Hour 20 Minutes
Start to Finish: 2 Hours 50 Minutes
About 4 dozen cookies

COOKIES

½ cup butter, softened
½ cup vegetable shortening

1 cup powdered sugar
1 egg
1½ teaspoons vanilla
2½ cups Gold Medal all-purpose flour
½ cup unsweetened baking cocoa
1 teaspoon salt

CHOCOLATE GLAZE

2 oz unsweetened baking chocolate
2 tablespoons butter
2 cups powdered sugar
3 to 4 tablespoons water
¼ cup crushed hard peppermint candy

1 Heat oven to 375°F.

2 In large bowl, mix ½ cup butter, the shortening, 1 cup powdered sugar, the egg, and vanilla until well blended. Stir in flour, cocoa, and salt.

3 Working with 1 level tablespoon of dough at a time, knead with hands until pliable and easy to mold. On surface lightly dusted with flour, roll dough into 9-inch pencil-like log. To make pretzel shape, form rope into a circle, crossing ends leaving 1½ inches free. Fold ends down to bottom of circle; press into circle. Onto each of 2 ungreased cookie sheets, arrange 12 cookies 1 inch apart.

4 Bake 1 cookie sheet about 9 minutes or until set. Cool 1 to 2 minutes; remove from cookie sheet to cooling rack. Repeat with second cookie sheet.

5 Onto completely cooled cookie sheets, continue forming and baking cookies as directed in Steps 3 and 4.

6 In microwavable medium bowl, heat baking chocolate and 2 tablespoons butter on High 45 seconds; stir until mixture can be stirred smooth. Add 2 cups powdered sugar and 3 tablespoons water; beat with spoon until smooth. Add additional water, 1 teaspoon at a time, until smooth and drizzling consistency.

7 Dip tops of cookies into glaze; place on cooling rack. Sprinkle with peppermint candy. Let stand until set.

How to Store: Let these cookies set or harden before storing. Store loosely wrapped by placing cookies between layers of parchment or waxed paper, plastic wrap, or foil at room temperature.

1 Cookie Calories 110; Total Fat 5g (Saturated Fat 2.5g, Trans Fat 0g); Cholesterol 10mg; Sodium 70mg; Total Carbohydrate 14g (Dietary Fiber 0g); Protein 1g **Carbohydrate Choices:** 1

Our *Betty Crocker's Cook Book for Boys and Girls* originally debuted in 1957 and since then has had several reprints and a facsimile version published. It still remains a favorite, helping kids learn to cook with a retro vibe.

These sweet little oval cookies, which Anna S. remembers from school lunches and most likely made by caring lunch ladies, were a joy to re-create. She told us they were "soft cookies with cherries in them, shaped like an egg."

Soft Cherry Cookies

Prep Time: 30 Minutes
Start to Finish: 1 Hour 15 Minutes
About 5½ dozen cookies

⅔ cup butter, softened
⅔ cup shortening

1½ cups granulated sugar
2 tablespoons maraschino cherry juice (from jar of maraschino cherries)
½ teaspoon almond extract
2 eggs

1½ cups maraschino cherries, chopped
3¾ cups Gold Medal all-purpose flour
1 teaspoon baking powder
¾ teaspoon salt
Powdered sugar, if desired

1 Heat oven to 350°F.

2 In large bowl, beat butter, shortening, sugar, maraschino cherry juice, almond extract, and eggs with electric mixer on medium speed until blended. Stir in maraschino cherries with spoon. Add flour, baking powder, and salt; beat with electric mixer on low speed just until mixed. Cover; refrigerate dough at least 2 hours.

3 Shape dough by rounded measuring tablespoonfuls into ovals about 1¾×1¼ inches. Onto each of 2 ungreased cookie sheets, arrange 12 ovals about 2 inches apart.

4 Bake 1 cookie sheet 8 to 10 minutes or until cookies are set when lightly touched.

Cool 3 minutes; remove from cookie sheets to cooling racks. Repeat with second cookie sheet.

5 Onto completely cooled cookie sheets, continue forming and baking cookies as directed in Steps 3 and 4.

6 Cool cookies completely, about 10 minutes. Sprinkle lightly with powdered sugar.

How to Store: Store at room temperature in tightly covered container.

Kitchen Notes: These cookies were tricky to get the texture right, without them being too soft or too floury tasting. We tried them with shortening or butter, but landed on a combination of both, for the best texture and flavor.

1 Cookie Calories 90; Total Fat 4g (Saturated Fat 1.5g, Trans Fat 0g); Cholesterol 10mg; Sodium 35mg; Total Carbohydrate 12g (Dietary Fiber 0g); Protein 1g **Carbohydrate Choices:** 1

Macaroons are typically made with almond paste or ground almonds mixed with sugar and egg whites. We love this vintage recipe for its tasty ingredients that go so well together . . . especially when topped with a chocolate glaze!

Almond-Cherry Macaroons

Prep Time: 15 Minutes
Start to Finish: 1 Hour
  15 Minutes
About 3 dozen cookies

COOKIES
1¼ cups coarsely chopped
  slivered almonds, toasted*
¾ cup sugar
3 egg whites
⅓ cup chopped maraschino
  cherries, well drained

GLAZE
1 oz unsweetened baking
  chocolate
1 teaspoon butter
1 cup powdered sugar
5 or 6 teaspoons boiling water

1 Heat oven to 300°F. Line 2 cookie sheets with cooking parchment paper.

2 In 2-quart saucepan, mix almonds, sugar, and egg whites. Cook over medium heat about 6 minutes, stirring constantly, until a path remains when a spoon is drawn through mixture; remove from heat. Stir in cherries; cool slightly.

3 Drop mixture by rounded teaspoonfuls about 2 inches apart onto parchment paper.

4 Bake 1 cookie sheet about 20 minutes or until light brown. Slide parchment paper and cookies onto cooling rack. Repeat with second cookie sheet. Cool cookies completely before peeling off parchment paper.

5 Onto completely cooled cookie sheet lined with cooking parchment paper, continue forming and baking cookies as directed in Steps 3 and 4.

6 In 2-quart saucepan, heat chocolate and butter over low heat until melted, stirring occasionally. Stir in powdered sugar and enough boiling water until thin enough to drizzle. Drizzle over cookies.

* To toast almonds: Heat oven to 350°F. Spread almonds in ungreased shallow pan. Bake uncovered 6 to 10 minutes, stirring occasionally, until light brown.

How to Store: Let cookies stand until glaze is set, about 2 hours. Store in tightly covered container at room temperature with waxed paper between layers.

1 Cookie Calories 70; Total Fat 3g (Saturated Fat 0g, Trans Fat 0g); Cholesterol 0mg; Sodium 5mg; Total Carbohydrate 9g (Dietary Fiber 0g); Protein 1g **Carbohydrate Choices:** ½

1957 package of Betty Crocker Coconut Macaroon Mix.

Betty Crocker
®

Coconut
Macaroon
MIX

Add only water

13 OZ. NET WT.

General Mills

Walnut and orange are a great flavor combination that you don't see much these days. Direct from our 1993 *Baking with Love* magazine, these delicious treats would be a welcome addition to any potluck or gathering.

Walnut-Orange Bars

Prep Time: 20 Minutes
Start to Finish: 2 Hours
   5 Minutes
36 bars

COOKIE BASE
¾ cup butter, softened
¾ cup powdered sugar
¼ cup unsweetened
   baking cocoa

1½ cups Gold Medal
   all-purpose flour

TOPPING
½ cup orange marmalade
1½ cups finely chopped walnuts
¾ cup packed brown sugar
¼ cup Gold Medal
   all-purpose flour
1 teaspoon vanilla
½ teaspoon baking powder

¼ teaspoon salt
2 eggs

CHOCOLATE FROSTING
2 tablespoons butter
2 tablespoons light corn syrup
2 tablespoons water
2 oz unsweetened baking
   chocolate
¾ to 1 cup powdered sugar

1 Heat oven to 375°F.

2 In medium bowl, mix ¾ cup butter, ¾ cup powdered sugar, and the cocoa. Stir in 1½ cups flour. Press dough evenly in ungreased 13×9-inch pan.

3 Bake about 10 minutes or just until edges begin to pull away from sides of pan. Spread marmalade over baked layer. In medium bowl, mix remaining topping ingredients; spread over marmalade.

4 Bake 20 to 25 minutes or until no indentation remains when touched in center. Cool completely in pan on cooling rack, about 1 hour.

5 In 1-quart saucepan, heat 2 tablespoons butter, the corn syrup, and water to boiling; remove from heat. Add chocolate, stirring until melted. Stir in enough powdered sugar until smooth and spreadable. Spread frosting over bars. Cut into 3 rows by 12 rows.

How to Store: Store these bars in a tightly covered container at room temperature.

1 Bar Calories 170; Total Fat 9g (Saturated Fat 3.5g, Trans Fat 0g); Cholesterol 20mg; Sodium 60mg; Total Carbohydrate 20g (Dietary Fiber 1g); Protein 2g **Carbohydrate Choices:** 1

These days, we typically title recipes with the main flavors it has in it, so you get a sense of what the recipe is. The flavors of toffee and nuts came together in this recipe from *Betty Crocker's Classics Recipe Cards*, with the name "Dream Bars." Once we tried them, we realized we shouldn't mess with perfection!

Dream Bars

Prep Time: 15 Minutes
Start to Finish: 1 Hour 10 Minutes
32 bars

BARS
⅓ cup butter, softened
⅓ cup packed brown sugar

1 cup Gold Medal all-purpose flour

ALMOND-COCONUT TOPPING
2 eggs
1 cup coconut
1 cup chopped almonds

¾ cup packed brown sugar
2 tablespoons Gold Medal all-purpose flour
1 teaspoon baking powder
1 teaspoon vanilla
¼ teaspoon salt

1 Heat oven to 350°F.

2 In small bowl, mix butter and ⅓ cup brown sugar with spoon until well blended. Stir in 1 cup flour. Press in ungreased 13×9-inch pan. Bake 10 minutes.

3 Meanwhile, in medium bowl, beat eggs with fork. Stir in remaining topping ingredients. Spread topping over baked layer.

4 Bake 20 to 25 minutes or until topping is golden brown. Cool 30 minutes. While warm, cut into 8 rows by 4 rows.

How to Store: Store these bars tightly covered in the refrigerator.

1 Bar Calories 110; Total Fat 5g (Saturated Fat 2.5g, Trans Fat 0g); Cholesterol 15mg; Sodium 60mg; Total Carbohydrate 13g (Dietary Fiber 0g); Protein 1g **Carbohydrate Choices:** 1

These yummy three-layer bars blend the flavors of brown sugar, coconut, walnuts, and citrus together to create a unique sweet your taste buds will appreciate. We grabbed them from our 1969 *Betty Crocker Cookbook* to put them at the top of our recipe box once again.

Coconut Chews

Prep Time: 25 Minutes
Start to Finish: 3 Hours
32 bars

COOKIE BASE
¾ cup powdered sugar
½ cup butter, softened
¼ cup vegetable shortening
1½ cups Gold Medal all-purpose or whole wheat flour

FILLING
½ cup chopped walnuts
½ cup coconut
2 tablespoons Gold Medal all-purpose or whole wheat flour
1 tablespoon packed brown sugar
½ teaspoon baking powder
½ teaspoon salt
½ teaspoon vanilla
2 eggs

CITRUS FROSTING
1½ cups powdered sugar
2 tablespoons butter, melted
3 tablespoons fresh orange juice
1 tablespoon fresh lemon juice

1 Heat oven to 350°F.

2 In medium bowl, mix powdered sugar, butter, and shortening until well mixed. Stir in 1½ cups flour. Press in bottom of ungreased 13×9-inch pan. Bake 12 to 15 minutes or until golden brown.

3 In medium bowl, mix the filling ingredients until well blended. Spread over baked layer.

4 Bake 20 minutes. Cool completely in pan on cooling rack, about 2 hours.

5 In small bowl, mix all frosting ingredients until smooth and spreading consistency. Spread over bars. Cut into 8 rows by 4 rows.

Pecan Chews: Substitute 1 cup chopped pecans for the walnuts and coconut.

How to Store: Store these bars tightly covered in the refrigerator.

1 Bar Calories 130; Total Fat 7g (Saturated Fat 3.5g, Trans Fat 0g); Cholesterol 20mg; Sodium 80mg; Total Carbohydrate 15g (Dietary Fiber 0g); Protein 1g **Carbohydrate Choices:** 1

From our 1988 *Christmas Cookbook*, these crunchy bars with the unique shape are a hit with young and old alike. They're a great choice as part of your holiday cookie tray, for a picnic, or after-school treat.

Chocolate-Almond-Toffee Triangles

Prep Time: 15 Minutes
Start to Finish: 2 Hours
   45 Minutes
48 bars

1 cup butter, softened
½ cup granulated sugar
½ cup packed brown sugar
1 egg
1 teaspoon vanilla

2 cups Gold Medal
  all-purpose flour
¼ teaspoon salt
1 cup milk chocolate chips
¾ cup toffee bits

1 Heat oven to 350°F.

2 In large bowl, mix butter, granulated sugar, brown sugar, egg, and vanilla until well blended. Stir in flour and salt. With floured hands, press dough in ungreased 15×10×1-inch pan.

3 Bake about 25 minutes or until light brown. Immediately sprinkle chocolate chips on hot crust. Let stand about 5 minutes or until chocolate is soft; spread evenly. Sprinkle with toffee bits. Place pan on cooling rack; let cool until chocolate is set, about 2 hours.

4 Cut into 6 rows by 4 rows; cut bars diagonally in half.

Almond-Cardamom Triangles: Make as directed, except add 1 teaspoon ground cardamom with the flour. Substitute ½ cup chopped toasted almonds for the toffee bits.

How to Store: Store these cooled bars in tightly covered container at room temperature.

1 Bar Calories 120; Total Fat 7g (Saturated Fat 4g, Trans Fat 0g); Cholesterol 20mg; Sodium 25mg; Total Carbohydrate 14g (Dietary Fiber 0g); Protein 1g **Carbohydrate Choices:** 1

We're sure our food stylists today would gasp at this photo shoot from 1964. Not only did the shoot require several cakes to be styled and held under the hot lights (without the frostings melting), but the shoot happened near the floor, making it physically difficult to work on the food. And one of the cakes also had *lit* candles on it, adding to the complexity of the shot.

These cute bars were one of the very first recipes to exist in our recipe database. Still creating recipes for our consumers today, to date we have made it to nearly 96,000 recipes in the database. As always, they are still thoroughly tested by culinary professionals to make them easy to follow with sweet success.

Strawberry Cheesecake Bars

Prep Time: 20 Minutes
Start to Finish: 5 Hours
36 bars

2 cups Gold Medal all-purpose flour
½ cup powdered sugar
⅔ cup cold butter

2 packages (8 oz each) cream cheese or ⅓-less-fat cream cheese (Neufchâtel), softened
½ cup granulated sugar
2 eggs
1 cup frozen (thawed) sliced strawberries with sugar (from a 15-oz container)

Sliced fresh strawberries or additional frozen (thawed) sliced strawberries with sugar, if desired
Basil or mint leaves, if desired

1 Heat oven to 350°F.

2 In medium bowl, mix flour and powdered sugar. Cut in butter with fork until mixture resembles fine crumbs. Press firmly and evenly into bottom of ungreased 13×9-inch pan. Bake 15 minutes.

3 In medium bowl, beat cream cheese with electric mixer on medium speed until smooth and fluffy. Beat in granulated sugar and eggs. Stir in strawberries (with syrup). Spread cream cheese mixture over baked layer.

4 Bake 20 to 25 minutes or just until center is set. Cool completely in pan on cooling rack. Cover loosely and refrigerate about 4 hours or until firm.

5 Cut into 4 rows by 9 rows. Refrigerate any remaining bars. Garnish with sliced fresh strawberries and basil.

How to Store: Store bars in pan tightly covered in refrigerator.

1 Bar Calories 130; Total Fat 8g (Saturated Fat 5g, Trans Fat 0g); Cholesterol 30mg; Sodium 45mg; Total Carbohydrate 12g (Dietary Fiber 0g); Protein 2g **Carbohydrate Choices:** 1

These delicious bars are appropriately named, as they do melt in your mouth, deliciously! From *Betty Crocker's Buffets* cookbook (1984), these are perfect for a large gathering such as a graduation, shower, or potluck.

No-Bake Fudge Meltaways

Prep Time: 15 Minutes
Start to Finish: 4 Hours
   15 Minutes
36 bars

BARS
½ cup butter
1½ oz unsweetened baking
   chocolate
1¾ cups graham cracker
   crumbs (about 28 squares)
1 cup coconut
½ cup chopped nuts
¼ cup granulated sugar
2 tablespoons water
1 teaspoon vanilla

FROSTING
2 cups powdered sugar
¼ cup butter, softened
3 tablespoons milk
1 teaspoon vanilla
1½ oz unsweetened baking
   chocolate

1 Line 9-inch square pan with foil. In 3-quart saucepan, heat ½ cup butter and 1½ ounces baking chocolate over medium heat until melted. Remove from heat. Stir in remaining bar ingredients. Press into pan. Refrigerate while making frosting.

2 In medium bowl, mix powdered sugar and ¼ cup butter until smooth. Stir in milk and vanilla. Spread over bars. Place 1½ ounces baking chocolate in microwavable custard cup. Microwave on High 30 seconds; stir until smooth. Spread evenly over frosting.

3 Cover and refrigerate 2 hours (bars will continue to get hard if left in the refrigerator longer than 2 hours, making them difficult to cut). Lift bars with foil from pan; fold back foil. Cut into 6 rows by 6 rows. Cover and refrigerate at least 2 hours longer but no longer than 48 hours.

How to Store: Store these bars in an airtight container in the refrigerator.

1 Bar Calories 120; Total Fat 7g (Saturated Fat 4g, Trans Fat 0g); Cholesterol 10mg; Sodium 60mg; Total Carbohydrate 13g (Dietary Fiber 0g); Protein 1g **Carbohydrate Choices:** 1

Direct from the pages of our 1990 *Perfect Baking Every Time* magazine, these homey bars bring a bit of coziness in every bite.

Walnut-Cinnamon Crisps

Prep Time: 15 Minutes
Start to Finish: 40 Minutes
48 bars

1 cup sugar
1 cup butter, softened
1 egg, separated
2 cups Gold Medal
    all-purpose flour

½ teaspoon ground cinnamon
1 tablespoon water
½ cup very finely chopped
    walnuts

1 Heat oven to 350°F. Grease 15×10×1-inch pan with vegetable shortening or spray with cooking spray.

2 In medium bowl, mix sugar, butter, and egg yolk until well blended. Stir in flour and cinnamon. Press lightly in pan. In small bowl, beat egg white and water with whisk or fork until foamy; brush over dough. Sprinkle with walnuts.

3 Bake 20 to 25 minutes or until very light brown. Immediately cut into 6 rows by 4 rows. Cut pieces diagonally into halves. Remove from pan to cooling rack. Store loosely covered at room temperature.

1 Bar Calories 80; Total Fat 5g (Saturated Fat 2.5g, Trans Fat 0g); Cholesterol 15mg; Sodium 0mg; Total Carbohydrate 8g (Dietary Fiber 0g); Protein 1g
Carbohydrate Choices: ½

Home economists not only created and tested new recipes and products but also other kitchen and home goods and appliances.

In the Betty Crocker Experimental Kitchen, the new "release" paper is being tested for effectiveness. Yes, the macaroons come up without any sticking at all!

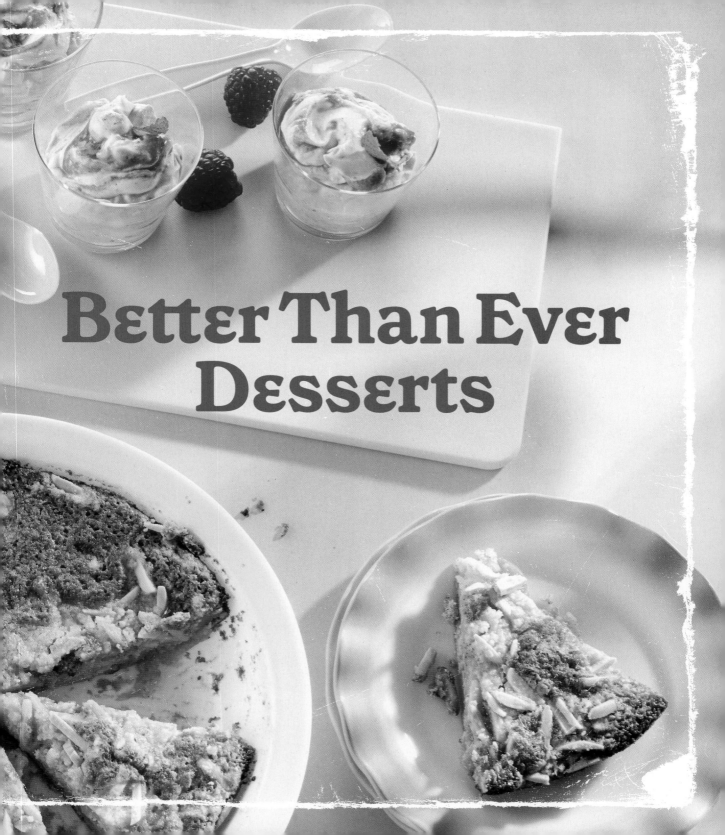

Better Than Ever Desserts

Loaded with the goodness of banana and zucchini, this is the perfect vintage snack cake to have on the counter for your family to "nibble" on. It's moist and packed with flavor. It would be equally perfect to take to a potluck!

Zucchini–Chocolate Chip– Banana Cake

Prep Time: 25 Minutes
Start to Finish: 2 Hours
   10 Minutes
12 servings

CAKE
2¼ cups Gold Medal
   all-purpose flour
1⅓ cups granulated sugar
⅔ cup miniature semisweet
   chocolate chips
1 cup mashed bananas
   (from 2 to 3 medium)
¾ cup shredded zucchini
⅔ cup butter, softened
⅔ cup buttermilk
1¼ teaspoons baking powder
1¼ teaspoons baking soda
¾ teaspoon salt
1 teaspoon vanilla
3 eggs

PEANUT BUTTER FROSTING
3 cups powdered sugar
⅓ cup creamy peanut butter
¼ cup plus 1 tablespoon milk
1½ teaspoons vanilla

1 Heat oven to 350°F. Grease 13×9-inch pan with vegetable shortening or spray with cooking spray; lightly flour.

2 In large bowl, beat all cake ingredients with electric mixer on low speed 1 minute or until dry ingredients are moistened, scraping bowl constantly. Beat on high speed 3 minutes, scraping bowl occasionally. Pour into pan.

3 Bake 38 to 42 minutes or until toothpick inserted in center comes out clean. Cool pan on cooling rack, about 1 hour.

4 In large bowl, mix powdered sugar and peanut butter with electric mixer on low speed until blended. Beat in ¼ cup of the milk and the vanilla. Gradually beat in just enough remaining milk, 1 teaspoon at a time, to make frosting smooth and spreadable. Frost cake. Cut cake into 3 rows by 4 rows.

1 Serving Calories 540; Total Fat 19g (Saturated Fat 10g, Trans Fat 0g); Cholesterol 75mg; Sodium 480mg; Total Carbohydrate 84g (Dietary Fiber 2g); Protein 7g **Carbohydrate Choices:** 5½

1¼ LBS. NET WT.

Betty Crocker ®
Cake Mix

CHOCOLATE DEVILS FOOD

You add *fresh* eggs and water

INGREDIENTS: Sugar, **Softasilk Cake Flour** (Bleached), vegetable shortening, cocoa, non-fat dry milk solids, leavening, salt, and artificial flavoring.
Mfd. by **General Mills, Inc.** General Offices, Minneapolis, Minnesota © GMI

 Betty Crocker says:

This package contains high quality ingredients for a wonderful SOFTASILK CAKE . . . a rich Devils Food cake with fresh egg goodness, because you add the eggs. We have found that fresh eggs give finer cakes most consistently. Be sure to follow directions EXACTLY.

FOR HIGH ALTITUDES SEE SIDE PANEL ➜

FIRST . . . Preheat oven to 350° (moderate) (325° for glass pans).
- Use two 8 or 9-in. round layer pans, at least 1¼-in. deep or 1 oblong pan, 13x9½x2-in.
- Grease pans generously and dust with flour.
- Measure 1 cup water. Have 2 unbeaten eggs ready.
- Empty package contents into large bowl.

THEN

BY HAND MIXING	BY ELECTRIC MIXER
1. **STIR** in ½ cup water and 1 unbeaten egg. Beat 2 minutes (about 150 strokes per minute). Scrape spoon and bowl often.	1. **BLEND** in ½ cup water and 1 unbeaten egg. Beat 2 minutes on medium (middle of dial) speed. (Guide batter into beaters and scrape sides and bottom of bowl often.)
2. **STIR** in gradually the remaining ½ cup water and 1 unbeaten egg. Beat another 2 minutes.	2. **BLEND** in remaining ½ cup water and 1 unbeaten egg. Beat another 2 minutes.

BAKE AT 350° { 8-in. layers, about 30 minutes
9-in. layers, about 25 minutes
oblong, about 35 minutes

KEYS TO SUCCESS:
Cake is done if it springs back when touched lightly in center.

Cool cake 10 minutes before removing from pan.

DEVILS FOOD CUPCAKES
Reduce water to ¾ cup, using only ¼ cup in the second addition of water. Set paper baking cups in muffin pans; fill scant ½ full. Bake at 400° (moderately hot oven) 15 to 18 minutes. Makes 24 medium-sized cupcakes.

 **CHOCOLATE DEVILS FOOD**
Cake Mix

Early cake mixes, like this one from 1952, had everything in the box except for water. Homemakers told us they wanted to add their own eggs to a mix, to give it that homemade experience.

Sherry D. remembered, "My family and neighbors loved this recipe since it wasn't dry, was very buttery tasting and I added raisins (which weren't on recipe)." We also loved this amazing pound cake when we tested it, and wholeheartedly agreed with Sherry's assessment. It's a winner!

Cream Cheese Pound Cake

Prep Time: 15 Minutes
Start to Finish: 2 Hours
  20 Minutes
16 servings

3½ cups Bisquick Original
  Pancake & Baking Mix
1½ cups granulated sugar
¾ cup butter, softened
¼ teaspoon salt
6 eggs

1 package (8 oz) cream cheese
  or ⅓-less-fat cream cheese
  (Neufchâtel), softened
Powdered sugar, if desired

1 Heat oven to 350°F. Grease 12-cup fluted tube cake pan or two 9×5-inch loaf pans with vegetable shortening or spray with cooking spray; lightly flour.

2 In large bowl, beat all ingredients except powdered sugar with electric mixer on low speed 30 seconds, scraping bowl frequently. Beat on medium speed 4 minutes, scraping bowl occasionally. Pour into pan(s).

3 Bake 55 to 65 minutes or until toothpick inserted near center comes out clean. Cool 5 minutes. Remove cake from pan(s) to cooling rack, top side up. Cool cake completely, about 1 hour. Sprinkle with powdered sugar.

Raisin Pound Cake: After mixing in Step 2, stir in 1 cup raisins.

Chocolate Chip Pound Cake: After mixing in Step 2, stir in 1 cup miniature chocolate chips.

1 Serving Calories 330; Total Fat 16g (Saturated Fat 9g, Trans Fat 0.5g); Cholesterol 105mg; Sodium 420mg; Total Carbohydrate 39g (Dietary Fiber 0g); Protein 5g **Carbohydrate Choices:** 2½

This deliciously sunny cake appeared in our *Gold Medal Century of Success* cookbook. Originally done as a layer cake, we've since updated the recipe with directions for making it in a 13×9 pan as well, making it totable for those times you want to bring dessert. The fresh orange flavor in both the cake and the frosting makes it truly exceptional with the nuts and raisins in the cake.

Williamsburg Orange Cake

Prep Time: 20 Minutes
Start to Finish: 2 Hours
  20 Minutes
16 servings

CAKE
2½ cups Gold Medal
  all-purpose flour
1½ cups sugar
¾ cup butter, softened

1½ cups buttermilk
1 tablespoon orange zest
1½ teaspoons baking soda
1½ teaspoons vanilla
¾ teaspoon salt
3 eggs
1 cup golden raisins,
  coarsely chopped
½ cup chopped nuts

ORANGE BUTTER FROSTING
⅓ cup butter, softened
3 cups powdered sugar
2 teaspoons orange zest
2 to 3 tablespoons fresh
  orange juice

1 Heat oven to 350°F. Grease 13×9-inch pan or 2 (9-inch) round cake pans with vegetable shortening or spray with cooking spray; lightly flour.

2 In large bowl, beat all cake ingredients with electric mixer on low speed 30 seconds, scraping bowl occasionally. Beat on high speed 3 minutes, scraping bowl occasionally. Pour into pan(s).

3 Bake 13×9-inch pan 40 to 50 minutes or round pans 30 to 35 minutes, or until toothpick inserted in center comes out clean. Cool 13×9-inch cake in pan on cooling rack; cool cake in round pans 10 minutes. Remove from pan(s) to cooling rack. Cool completely, about 1 hour.

4 In medium bowl, mix ⅓ cup butter and powdered sugar with electric mixer on low speed. Beat in 2 teaspoons orange zest and 2 tablespoons of the orange juice until blended. Add additional orange juice, 1 teaspoon at a time, until frosting is smooth and spreadable.

5 Frost top of 13×9-inch cake or fill and frost round layers with frosting.

Betty's Cooking Tip: Add whole-grain goodness by substituting 1¼ cups Gold Medal whole wheat flour for an equal amount of the all-purpose flour.

1 Serving Calories 430; Total Fat 17g (Saturated Fat 9g, Trans Fat 0.5g); Cholesterol 70mg; Sodium 270mg; Total Carbohydrate 65g (Dietary Fiber 1g); Protein 5g **Carbohydrate Choices:** 4

When Amy S. wrote asking for the recipe for Strawberry Poke Cake, we found we needed to re-create it since frozen strawberries in syrup are no longer available. So, we started with frozen plain strawberries and white Super Moist™ cake mix (because you can find it practically everywhere) but left the filling and topping intact as in the original recipe. We hope you love the fresh take on this memorable cake!

Fresh Strawberry-Pudding Poke Cake

Prep Time: 20 Minutes
Start to Finish: 2 Hours 10 Minutes
15 servings

1 package (15 oz) frozen strawberries, thawed

¼ cup sugar
2 teaspoons fresh lemon juice
1 box Betty Crocker Super Moist white cake mix
¾ cup water
½ cup vegetable oil
3 egg whites
3 to 4 drops red food color

1 cup milk
1 package (4-serving-size) vanilla instant pudding and pie filling mix
1 container (8 oz) frozen whipped topping, thawed
Sliced fresh strawberries, if desired

1 Heat oven to 350°F. Grease bottom of 13×9-inch pan with vegetable shortening or spray with cooking spray.

2 In food processor, process thawed frozen strawberries on high speed until smooth. Measure ½ cup strawberry puree; set aside. Add sugar and lemon juice to remaining strawberries and process until blended; set aside.

3 In large bowl, beat cake mix, the ½ cup reserved unsweetened strawberry puree, water, oil, egg whites, and food color with electric mixer on low speed 30 seconds. Beat on medium speed 2 minutes, scraping bowl occasionally. Pour into pan.

4 Bake 28 to 33 minutes or until toothpick inserted in center comes out clean. Cool on cooling rack 20 minutes.

5 Using the handle of a wooden spoon (¼ to ½ inch in diameter), poke holes about every inch almost to bottom of cake. Carefully pour reserved sweetened strawberry mixture over top of cake; spread with spatula to fill holes. Cool completely, about 1 hour.

6 In medium bowl, mix milk and pudding mix with whisk 2 minutes until thickened. Gently fold in whipped topping. Spread over cake. Cut into 5 rows by 3 rows. Garnish pieces with sliced fresh strawberries. Store any remaining cake loosely covered in refrigerator.

{ recipe continues }

Betty's Cooking Tip: If you are a real whipped cream lover, substitute 3 cups Sweetened Whipped Cream (page 227) for the frozen whipped topping.

Kitchen Notes: During testing and taste panels, we decided we wanted to be sure there was enough strawberry filling to get some in almost every bite. We poked more holes and added more filling, and the bright strawberry flavor came through beautifully!

1 Serving Calories 280; Total Fat 12g (Saturated Fat 4.5g, Trans Fat 0g); Cholesterol 0mg; Sodium 320mg; Total Carbohydrate 40g (Dietary Fiber 1g); Protein 3g **Carbohydrate Choices:** 2½

Lost Recipe Memory

"I first ate this cake when my daughter made it. It is soo good."

—Amy D.

On June 24, our home economist Marge Johnston baked 23 Betty Crocker cakes. Then she cut a thin slice out of every one. She did this to prove to the world, that all Betty Crocker cakes are so moist and rich bodied, you can slice them this thin without crumbling. Atta girl, Marge.

Betty Crocker cake mix advertisement from 1970.

Poke cakes, like this one, were first developed in the mid 1970s. Colorful fruit-flavored gelatin was poured over cake that had been poked with holes. The popularity of these cakes remains as other ingredients have been discovered to infuse cakes with flavor while also adding moistness.

Lemon–Poppy Seed Pound Cake

Prep Time: 25 Minutes
Start to Finish: 2 Hours
 40 Minutes
16 servings

CAKE
2½ cups Gold Medal
 all-purpose flour
1 teaspoon baking soda
½ teaspoon salt
1½ cups granulated sugar
½ cup butter, softened
3 eggs
1 cup buttermilk
¼ cup poppy seed
2 tablespoons lemon zest
2 tablespoons fresh lemon juice

LEMON GLAZE
2 cups powdered sugar
¼ cup butter, melted
2 tablespoons lemon zest
¼ cup lemon juice

1 Heat oven to 325°F. Generously grease 12-cup fluted tube cake pan with vegetable shortening or spray with cooking spray; lightly flour.

2 In medium bowl, mix flour, baking soda, and salt. In large bowl, beat granulated sugar and ½ cup butter with electric mixer on medium speed, scraping bowl frequently, until light and fluffy. Beat in eggs, one at a time.

3 Add flour mixture alternately with buttermilk beating on low speed, scraping bowl occasionally, until flour is moistened. Stir in poppy seed, lemon zest, and 2 tablespoons lemon juice.

4 Bake 50 to 55 minutes or until toothpick inserted in center comes out clean.

5 Meanwhile, in medium bowl, mix all lemon glaze ingredients until smooth; cover and set aside.

6 Immediately poke several holes in top of cake with long-tined fork. Stir glaze; slowly pour about two-thirds of the lemon glaze over top of cake. Cover and reserve remaining glaze.

7 Cool cake in pan on cooling rack 20 minutes. Invert cake onto heatproof serving plate; remove pan. Cool cake completely, about 1 hour. Spread top with remaining glaze, allowing some to drizzle down side. Store any remaining cake loosely covered at room temperature.

1 Serving Calories 320; Total Fat 11g (Saturated Fat 6g, Trans Fat 0g); Cholesterol 60mg; Sodium 250mg; Total Carbohydrate 51g (Dietary Fiber 1g); Protein 4g **Carbohydrate Choices:** 3½

Heralded as the "cake discovery of the century" in 1947, chiffon cake recipes were created and tested in the Betty Crocker Kitchens and became popular at dinner parties across the country. What made this cake different from others? Most notably, it was the addition of salad (vegetable) oil.

Spice Chiffon Cake

Prep Time: 20 Minutes
Start to Finish: 3 Hours
    30 Minutes
12 servings

2 cups Gold Medal
    all-purpose flour
1½ cups sugar

3 teaspoons baking powder
1 teaspoon salt
½ cup vegetable oil
7 eggs, separated
¾ cup cold water
2 tablespoons caraway seed,
    if desired

1 teaspoon ground cinnamon
½ teaspoon ground nutmeg
½ teaspoon ground allspice
½ teaspoon ground cloves
½ teaspoon cream of tartar
Chocolate Joy Icing (below),
    if desired

1 Heat oven to 325°F.

2 In medium bowl, mix flour, sugar, baking powder, and salt. Make a well in the center of mixture; add oil, egg yolks, water, and spices. Beat with electric mixer on medium, scraping bowl frequently, 2 minutes or until smooth.

3 In large bowl, place egg whites and cream of tartar. Beat with electric mixer on high speed until stiff peaks form. Do not underbeat. Pour flour mixture in thin stream over entire surface of egg whites; gently fold into egg whites just until fully blended. Pour into ungreased 10-inch angel food (tube) cake pan.

4 Bake 55 minutes. Increase oven temperature to 350°F. Continue baking 10 to 15 minutes or until surface springs back when touched lightly. Immediately turn pan upside down onto heatproof bottle or funnel. Let hang about 2 hours or until cake is completely cool.

5 Loosen side of cake with knife or long metal spatula; remove from pan. Drizzle icing over top of cake, allowing some to drip down side.

Chocolate Joy Icing: In medium bowl, mix 2⅔ cups powdered sugar, ¼ cup unsweetened baking cocoa, and ¼ teaspoon salt. Add ⅓ cup vegetable shortening, 1 tablespoon corn syrup, and 3 tablespoons hot water. Beat with electric mixer on low speed, scraping bowl occasionally, until smooth. Add additional hot water, 1 teaspoon at a time, until smooth and drizzling consistency.

Chocolate Chip Chiffon Cake: Prepare as directed, except increase sugar to 1¾ cups. Omit caraway seed, cinnamon, nutmeg, allspice, and cloves. Before pouring batter into pan, sprinkle 3 oz grated semisweet baking chocolate over batter; gently fold into batter with 2 or 3 strokes.

1 Serving Calories 300; Total Fat 12g (Saturated Fat 2.5g, Trans Fat 0g); Cholesterol 110mg; Sodium 360mg; Total Carbohydrate 42g (Dietary Fiber 0g); Protein 6g **Carbohydrate Choices:** 3

Chiffon cake recipe booklet circa 1953.

Who was Bonnie and why did she get a cake named after her? We think this cake was actually named for the use of the word in the Scottish language, meaning "attractive or good." It appeared in the 1969 version of *Betty Crocker's Cookbook*, and its rich, homemade flavor is still a "bonnie" favorite of ours. You can decorate it with your favorite candy sprinkles to suit any occasion.

Bonnie Butter Cake

Prep Time: 20 Minutes
Start to Finish: 2 Hours
  20 Minutes
12 servings

BUTTER CAKE
2¾ cups Gold Medal
  all-purpose flour

2½ teaspoons baking powder
1 teaspoon salt
⅔ cup butter, softened
1¾ cups granulated sugar
2 eggs
1½ teaspoons vanilla
1¼ cups milk

CHOCOLATE BUTTER FROSTING
½ cup butter, softened
4 oz unsweetened baking
  chocolate, melted, cooled
4½ cups powdered sugar
1 tablespoon vanilla
3 to 4 tablespoons milk

1 Heat oven to 350°F. Grease 13×9-inch pan or 2 (9-inch) round cake pans with vegetable shortening or spray with cooking spray; lightly flour.

2 In medium bowl, mix flour, baking powder, and salt; set aside. In large bowl, mix ⅔ cup butter, the granulated sugar, eggs, and 1½ teaspoons vanilla with electric mixer on low speed, scraping bowl constantly, about 2 minutes or until light and fluffy. Beat on high speed, scraping bowl occasionally, 5 minutes. On low speed, alternately add flour mixture, about one-third of mixture at a time, and milk, about half at a time. Beat on high speed 3 minutes. Pour into pan(s).

3 Bake 13×9-inch pan 45 to 50 minutes or round pans 30 to 35 minutes or until toothpick inserted in center comes out clean. Cool 13×9-inch cake completely in pan on cooling rack; cool rounds in pans 10 minutes. Remove from pans to cooling rack. Cool completely, about 1 hour.

4 In large bowl, beat ½ cup butter and melted chocolate with electric mixer on low speed until blended. Gradually beat in powdered sugar until blended. Beat in vanilla and 3 tablespoons of the milk. Add additional milk, 1 teaspoon at a time, beating on low speed until frosting is smooth and spreadable. Frost top of 13×9-inch cake or fill and frost layers with frosting.

1 Serving Calories 650; Total Fat 25g (Saturated Fat 15g, Trans Fat 0.5g); Cholesterol 80mg; Sodium 470mg; Total Carbohydrate 101g (Dietary Fiber 2g); Protein 6g **Carbohydrate Choices:** 7

Butterscotch and marshmallow were popular flavors in desserts in decades past, and this recipe was on top of the list to appear in the 1992 *Betty Crocker's Old-Fashioned Desserts* cookbook. You can't go wrong with these flavors in a rich, moist chocolate cake. Every bite and every "mmm" from family and friends will tell you it was worth the effort!

Chocolate Buttermallow Cake

Prep Time: 55 Minutes
Start to Finish: 1 Hour
  55 Minutes
12 servings

CAKE

1¾ cups Gold Medal
  all-purpose flour or 2 cups
  cake flour
1 cup granulated sugar
½ cup packed brown sugar
1½ teaspoons baking soda
¾ teaspoon salt
1¼ cups buttermilk

½ cup vegetable shortening
2 eggs
1 teaspoon vanilla
½ teaspoon red liquid
  food color
2 oz unsweetened baking
  chocolate, melted, cooled

BUTTERSCOTCH FILLING

½ cup packed brown sugar
¼ cup cornstarch
¼ teaspoon salt
½ cup water
1 tablespoon butter

½ cup chopped nuts

MARSHMALLOW FROSTING

1 egg white
¾ cup granulated sugar
⅛ teaspoon cream of tartar
1½ teaspoons light corn syrup
3 tablespoons water
¼ cup plus 2 tablespoons
  marshmallow creme
  (from 7-oz jar)

1 oz semisweet baking chocolate

1 Heat oven to 350°F. Grease bottoms and sides of 2 (9-inch) round cake pans with vegetable shortening or spray with cooking spray; lightly flour.

2 In large bowl, beat all cake ingredients except food color and melted chocolate with electric mixer on low speed 45 seconds, scraping bowl constantly. Beat in food color and 2 ounces melted chocolate on high speed 3 minutes, scraping bowl occasionally. Pour into pans.

3 Bake 25 to 30 minutes or until toothpick inserted in center comes out clean. Cool 10 minutes; remove from pans to cooling rack. Cool completely, about 1 hour.

4 Meanwhile, in 1-quart saucepan, mix brown sugar, cornstarch, and salt. Stir in water. Cook, stirring constantly until mixture thickens and boils. Boil and stir 1 minute; stir in butter. Cool butterscotch filling to room temperature.

5 Place 1 cake layer, bottom side up, on plate. Spread with half of the butterscotch filling to within ½ inch of edge; sprinkle with half of the nuts. Top with remaining cake layer, bottom side down, on top of nuts. Spread remaining butterscotch filling on top of cake (reserve remaining nuts for top of cake).

6 In 2-quart saucepan, mix all marshmallow frosting ingredients except marshmallow creme. Cook over low heat, beating continuously with electric hand mixer at high speed until soft peaks form. Add marshmallow creme; beat until stiff peaks form. Remove from heat.

7 Frost sides and top of cake with frosting. In small microwavable bowl, microwave half of the chocolate on High, about 30 seconds, or until chocolate can be stirred smooth. Cool slightly. Dip back of spoon in chocolate; press gently into frosting on top of cake and twist to swirl. Repeat with remaining melted chocolate. Chop remaining chocolate. Sprinkle cake with remaining ¼ cup nuts and chocolate.

1 Serving Calories 470; Total Fat 17g (Saturated Fat 6g, Trans Fat 0g); Cholesterol 35mg; Sodium 430mg; Total Carbohydrate 72g (Dietary Fiber 2g); Protein 6g **Carbohydrate Choices:** 5

A traditional dessert in Germany for many special occasions, such as weddings and anniversaries, Black Forest desserts seemed to pop up everywhere in the US during the '80s and early '90s. This flavor-packed cake, which appeared in our *Century of Success Cookbook*, is still our favorite take on the classic torte.

Black Forest Cherry Torte

Prep Time: 1 Hour
Start to Finish: 2 Hours
   30 Minutes
12 servings

Bonnie Butter Cake (page 214)

CHERRY FILLING

2 tablespoons cornstarch

2 tablespoons granulated sugar

1 can (15 oz) pitted sweet dark
   cherries

1 tablespoon brandy or
   brandy flavoring

TOPPINGS

1½ cups heavy whipping cream

¼ cup powdered sugar

⅓ bar (4.4-oz-size) milk- or
   dark-chocolate candy bar,
   grated

1 Prepare Bonnie Butter Cake in 9-inch layers as directed through Step 3 (do not prepare the frosting).

2 Meanwhile, in 1-quart saucepan, mix cornstarch and granulated sugar. Drain cherries, reserving syrup. Add enough water to reserved cherry syrup to measure 1 cup; stir into cornstarch mixture. Cook over medium-high heat, stirring constantly, until mixture thickens and boils. Boil and stir 1 minute. Cool to lukewarm. Stir in brandy.

3 Line plate with cooking parchment paper. Dip 36 cherries in thickened syrup; place on lined plate. Reserve for top of cake. Cut remaining cherries into fourths; stir in thickened syrup.

4 Place 1 cake layer, bottom side up, on serving plate. In medium bowl, beat whipping cream and powdered sugar with electric mixer on low speed until mixture begins to thicken. Gradually increase speed to high and beat until stiff peaks form. Using a decorating bag fitted with a star tip or spoon, pipe a thin border of whipped cream around edge of layer on plate. Spoon cherry filling inside border. Place other layer, bottom side down, on filling. Gently spread whipped cream on side and top of cake. Gently press grated chocolate, by teaspoonfuls, onto side of cake.

5 Place remaining whipped cream in decorating bag fitted with star tip. Pipe border of whipped cream around top edge of cake. Spoon reserved cherries inside border. Store cake in refrigerator until ready to serve. Loosely wrap any remaining cake and store in refrigerator.

Easy Black Forest Cherry Torte: Omit Bonnie Butter Cake. Prepare, bake, and cool Betty Crocker Super Moist yellow cake mix as directed on package for 2 (9-inch) layers. Continue as directed in Step 2.

---

1 Serving Calories 500; Total Fat 22g (Saturated Fat 14g, Trans Fat 1g); Cholesterol 95mg; Sodium 420mg; Total Carbohydrate 67g (Dietary Fiber 2g); Protein 6g **Carbohydrate Choices:** 4½

Betty Crocker Classics dessert mixes, 1984.

Blushing Peach Pie recipe with Betty Crocker pie crust advertisement circa 1968.

Spice up Valentine's Day with Blushing Peach Pie
(put a little heart in it)

Betty Crocker Pie Crust and Cling Peaches
have a love affair with cinnamon hearts

This rosy-colored, cinnamony peach pie appeared in our cookbooks back in the '90s. With the insanely pretty color and flavor of the filling, we just had to bring it back to the top of our loved recipes list. Our editor believes no fruit pie should be served by itself, so top it with sweetened whipped cream or ice cream, for the ultimate homemade pie-eating experience.

Blushing Peach Pie

Prep Time: 25 Minutes
Start to Finish: 3 Hours 15 Minutes
8 servings

Pie Pastry (page 222) for two-crust pie
6 cups sliced fresh peaches (6 to 8 medium) or 3 bags (10 oz each) drained thawed frozen peaches
½ cup sugar

¼ cup Gold Medal all-purpose flour
¼ cup red cinnamon candies
2 tablespoons butter
Sweetened Whipped Cream (page 227) or ice cream, if desired

1 Heat oven to 425°F. Prepare pastry dough and roll out both disks as directed. Place 1 pastry in 9-inch glass pie plate.

2 In large bowl, mix all remaining ingredients except butter and whipped cream. Spoon into pastry-lined pie plate. Dot with butter. Cover with top pastry; cut slits in pastry. Seal and flute edge as directed. Cover edge with 2- to 3-inch strips of foil to prevent excess browning.

3 Bake 40 to 50 minutes or until crust is golden brown and juice begins to bubble through slits in crust. Remove foil during last 15 minutes of baking. Cool on cooling rack at least 2 hours. Serve with sweetened whipped cream.

Betty's Cooking Tip: For a sparkly and sugary crust, before baking, brush the top pastry lightly with water. Sprinkle lightly with sugar. Watch carefully while baking. If dark spots appear, cover them loosely with small pieces of aluminum foil.

1 Serving Calories 440; Total Fat 21g (Saturated Fat 6g, Trans Fat 0g); Cholesterol 10mg; Sodium 320mg; Total Carbohydrate 58g (Dietary Fiber 3g); Protein 5g **Carbohydrate Choices:** 4

What's the secret to a fabulous tasting pie? A flaky crust that lets the filling take center stage. Shortening creates the perfect flaky texture while providing a neutral flavor. You'll love the results!

Pie Pastry

Prep Time: 20 Minutes
Start to Finish: 20 Minutes
8 servings

ONE-CRUST PASTRY

1 cup plus 1 tablespoon Gold Medal all-purpose flour

½ teaspoon salt

⅓ cup cold shortening

3 to 5 tablespoons ice-cold water

TWO-CRUST PASTRY

2 cups plus 2 tablespoons Gold Medal all-purpose flour

1 teaspoon salt

⅔ cup cold shortening

6 to 8 tablespoons ice-cold water

1 In medium bowl, mix flour and salt. Cut in shortening, using pastry blender or fork, until mixture forms coarse crumbs the size of small peas. Sprinkle with water, 1 tablespoon at a time, tossing with fork until all flour is moistened and pastry almost leaves side of bowl.

2 Gather pastry into a ball. For one-crust pastry, shape dough into flattened disk on lightly floured surface. For two-crust pastry, divide dough in half and flatten into 2 disks on lightly floured surface.

3 Using floured rolling pin, roll 1 disk of pastry on lightly floured surface into round 2 inches larger than upside-down 9-inch glass pie plate or 3 inches larger than 10- or 11-inch tart pan. Fold pastry into fourths and place in pie plate or tart pan. Unfold (or unroll) pastry and ease into plate or pan, pressing firmly against bottom and side and being careful not to stretch pastry, which will cause it to shrink when baked.

4 For one-crust pie, trim overhanging edge of pastry 1 inch from rim of pie plate. Fold edge under to form standing rim; flute edges. Fill and bake as directed in pie or tart recipe.

5 For two-crust pie, roll out second pastry disk. Fold into fourths and unfold over filling (or roll loosely around rolling pin and place over filling). Cut slits in pastry so steam can escape. Trim overhanging edge of top pastry 1 inch from rim of plate. Fold edge of top crust under bottom crust, forming a stand-up rim of pastry that is even thickness on edge of pie plate, pressing on rim to seal; flute edges. Bake as directed in pie recipe.

Butter Crust: Substitute cold butter, cut into ½-inch pieces, for half of the shortening. In Step 2, wrap rounds in plastic wrap and refrigerate 1 hour before continuing with Step 3.

1 Serving (One-Crust Pastry) Calories 140; Total Fat 9g (Saturated Fat 2g, Trans Fat 0g); Cholesterol 0mg; Sodium 150mg; Total Carbohydrate 13g (Dietary Fiber 0g); Protein 1g **Carbohydrate Choices:** 1

Baking Methods for Pie Crust

For many pies, such as apple or pecan pie, the filling is added to the unbaked pastry so that the crust and filling bake together at the same time. For other pies, such as pumpkin or banana cream pie, the crust is either partially baked or completely baked before the filling is added. This method is used either to prevent the crust from becoming soggy from liquid fillings or because the filling doesn't need to be baked.

Partially Baked One-Crust Pie

Use this when a recipe calls for a partially baked crust to prevent the bottom crust from becoming soggy, such as pumpkin pie.

1 Heat oven to 425°F. Prepare Pie Pastry (page 222) for one crust. Carefully cover pastry in plate with a double thickness of foil, gently pressing foil to bottom and side of pastry. Let foil extend over edge to prevent excessive browning.

2 Bake 10 minutes; carefully remove foil and bake 2 to 4 minutes longer or until pastry just begins to brown and has become set. If crust bubbles, gently push bubbles down with back of spoon while hot.

3 Fill and bake as directed in pie or tart recipe, changing oven temperature if necessary.

Baked One-Crust Pie

Use this for pies or tarts that call for a baked pastry before filling is added, such as lemon meringue pie.

1 Heat oven to 450°F. Prepare Pie Pastry (page 222) for one crust and roll out as directed. For pie, fit into pie plate and trim overhanging edge of pastry 1 inch from rim of pie plate. For tart, fit into tart pan and trim overhanging edge of pastry even with top of tart pan. Prick bottom and side of pastry thoroughly with fork to prevent puffing.

2 Bake 8 to 10 minutes or until light golden brown: cool on cooling rack.

3 Fill cooled crust as directed in pie or tart recipe.

Betty Crocker Pyequick pie crust advertisement circa 1949. The mix contained pie crust and apples. Homemakers only needed to add sugar and water.

Sugar pie is a rich, custard-like pie. It's simple to make with just a few ingredients. We love this one for how it forms its own layers. The use of rose water gives the pie a traditional Shaker influence, but vanilla could be used for equally delicious flavor. Variations on sugar pie were found from Indiana to New England to many Southern states.

Shaker Sugar Pie

Prep Time: 30 Minutes
Start to Finish: 2 Hours
    55 Minutes
12 servings

Pie Pastry (page 222) for
    one-crust pie
1 cup packed brown sugar
½ cup butter, softened
2 tablespoons Gold Medal
    all-purpose flour

1½ cups heavy whipping cream
1 teaspoon rose water or vanilla
1 egg
Ground nutmeg
Sugared Rose Petals (below),
    if desired

1 Heat oven to 450°F. Make pastry, roll out, and fit into 9-inch glass pie plate as directed; press edge with fork.

2 In small bowl, mix brown sugar, butter, and flour until well blended; spread in pastry shell. In medium bowl, beat whipping cream, rose water, and egg with whisk until well blended. Pour over brown sugar mixture. Sprinkle with nutmeg.

3 Bake 10 minutes. Reduce oven temperature to 350°F. Bake 25 to 30 minutes longer or until knife inserted in center comes out clean.

4 Cool on cooling rack 15 minutes. Refrigerate uncovered at least 2 hours or until chilled. Cover and refrigerate any remaining pie.

Sugared Rose Petals: Gently remove rose petals from one organic rose. Cut off white tips. Gently spritz both sides of petals with water; press gently with paper towel to dry. In small dish, beat 2 teaspoons dry meringue powder with 2 tablespoons water with fork until well blended. Working with one petal at a time, use a small pastry brush or clean paint brush to paint meringue powder mixture over both sides of petal. Over a small plate, sprinkle superfine sugar over both sides of petal to cover. Place on cooling rack to dry completely, about 1 hour. Use immediately or store uncovered at room temperature up to 3 days.

Betty's Cooking Tip: Rose water can be found in some larger grocery or discount stores or online. Be sure that you are using rose water intended for cooking purposes for this recipe.

1 Serving Calories 330; Total Fat 23g (Saturated Fat 12g, Trans Fat 0.5g); Cholesterol 70mg; Sodium 180mg; Total Carbohydrate 28g (Dietary Fiber 0g); Protein 2g **Carbohydrate Choices:** 2

When first introduced, pies like this one were called "Impossible Pies" because the Bisquick batter formed its own crust. No separate pastry was needed. Over the years, the recipes were renamed "Impossibly Easy Pies." Today, we have 268 recipes with 948 versions of sweet, savory, and even appetizers made with Bisquick in our recipe database.

Impossibly Easy Peaches 'n' Cream Pie

Prep Time: 15 Minutes
Start to Finish: 55 Minutes
8 servings

ALMOND STREUSEL
¼ cup Bisquick Original
   Pancake & Baking Mix
2 tablespoons sugar

1 tablespoon cold butter,
   cut into pieces
⅓ cup slivered almonds

PIE
2 cans (15 oz each) sliced
   peaches in juice, well drained,
   or 3 cups sliced peeled fresh
   peaches

½ teaspoon ground cinnamon
¼ teaspoon ground nutmeg
½ cup Bisquick Original
   Pancake & Baking Mix
½ cup sugar
¾ cup heavy whipping cream
2 eggs
Sweetened Whipped Cream
   (page 227), if desired

1 Heat oven to 375°F. Grease 9-inch pie plate with vegetable shortening or spray with cooking spray.

2 In small bowl, mix ¼ cup Bisquick mix and 2 tablespoons sugar. Cut in butter with fork until crumbly. Stir in almonds; set streusel aside.

3 Pat peaches dry with paper towels; place in pie plate. Sprinkle with cinnamon and nutmeg; toss until peaches are evenly coated.

4 In medium bowl, stir remaining pie ingredients except sweetened whipped cream with whisk until blended. Pour mixture into pie plate, lifting peaches to allow mixture to flow into pie plate. Sprinkle with streusel.

5 Bake 35 to 40 minutes or until knife inserted in center comes out clean. Serve warm or cold with whipped cream. Cover and refrigerate any remaining pie.

1 Serving Calories 260; Total Fat 13g (Saturated Fat 6g, Trans Fat 0g); Cholesterol 75mg; Sodium 140mg; Total Carbohydrate 32g (Dietary Fiber 1g); Protein 4g
Carbohydrate Choices: 2

Fan Memory
"It was easy and always a favorite at home!"
—Bernadette R.

Sweetened Whipped Cream

Sweetened whipped cream is the perfect touch on a piece of pie, cut-up fresh fruit, or even a coffee drink. This handy chart will help you know how much of each ingredient you'll need to make the amount of whipped cream you need.

Chill bowl and beaters in freezer or refrigerator 10 to 20 minutes. In chilled bowl, beat whipping cream, sugar, and vanilla with electric mixer on low speed until mixture begins to thicken. Gradually increase speed to high and beat just until soft peaks form. For stiffer whipped cream, beat just until stiff peaks form: Do not overbeat or mixture will curdle.

Yield	Bowl size	Heavy whipping cream	Sugar (powdered or granulated)	Vanilla
1 cup	medium	½ cup	1 tablespoon	½ teaspoon
2 cups	medium	1 cup	2 tablespoons	1 teaspoon
6 cups	large	3 cups	¼ cup plus 2 tablespoons	1 tablespoon

Meringue desserts were popular in the 1950s and 1960s. Many recipes for "chiffon" pies or other desserts called for folding uncooked meringues (raw egg whites and sugar) into fruit. We bring this sensational recipe back because of the three distinct and pretty layers, with the top layer being a baked meringue with coconut. It's fantastic.

Rhubarb-Meringue Squares

Prep Time: 20 Minutes
Start to Finish: 1 Hour
  25 Minutes
9 servings

CRUST
1 cup Gold Medal
  all-purpose flour

½ cup butter, softened
1 tablespoon sugar

RHUBARB FILLING
3 eggs
1 cup sugar
2 tablespoons Gold Medal
  all-purpose flour
¼ teaspoon salt

½ cup half-and-half
2½ cups (½- to 1-inch pieces)
  fresh rhubarb

MERINGUE
⅓ cup sugar
1 teaspoon vanilla
¼ cup coconut

1 Heat oven to 350°F.

2 In small bowl, mix all crust ingredients. Press into ungreased 9-inch square pan. Bake 10 minutes.

3 Separate eggs by placing egg whites in one medium bowl and egg yolks in another medium bowl. Cover and refrigerate egg whites. Add remaining rhubarb filling ingredients except rhubarb to egg yolks; mix well. Stir in rhubarb. Pour over baked layer.

4 Bake 45 minutes.

5 Uncover egg whites. Beat with electric mixer on high speed until foamy. Gradually add ⅓ cup sugar, 1 tablespoon at a time, beating until stiff peaks form and mixture is glossy. Do not underbeat. Beat in vanilla. Spread over hot rhubarb mixture, sprinkle with coconut.

6 Bake about 10 minutes or until coconut is light brown. Cut into 3 rows by 3 rows. Serve warm. Cover and refrigerate any remaining dessert.

1 Serving Calories 340; Total Fat 15g (Saturated Fat 9g, Trans Fat 0g); Cholesterol 95mg; Sodium 180mg; Total Carbohydrate 46g (Dietary Fiber 1g); Protein 4g **Carbohydrate Choices:** 3

Decadent, chocolaty recipes like this one could be found on restaurant dessert carts in the '80s and '90s. Tarts are like an open-faced pie—they only have a bottom crust! They are made in either a tart pan (with a removable bottom) or springform pan (which has a removable side) so you can remove the tart without damaging it. You might be tempted to skip the step of removing the skins from the hazelnuts, but don't! The bitter flavor of the skins would affect the rich, chocolaty flavor . . . and you'll want all the oohs and aahs that you'll get for your efforts.

Chocolate-Hazelnut Tart

Prep Time: 35 Minutes
Start to Finish: 1 Hour
  35 Minutes
12 servings

Pie Pastry (page 222) for
  one-crust pie
1/3 cup butter
2 oz unsweetened baking
  chocolate, chopped
3 eggs
2/3 cup sugar

1/2 teaspoon salt
1 cup light or dark corn syrup
1 cup toasted hazelnuts, skins
  removed* and coarsely
  chopped
Sweetened Whipped Cream
  (page 227), if desired

1 Move oven rack to lowest position. Heat oven to 475°F.

2 Prepare pie pastry as directed, except roll into 12-inch round. Gently fold pastry into fourths; unfold and ease into ungreased 9-inch springform pan, pressing firmly against bottom and 1¾ inches up side. Prick bottom and side thoroughly with fork.

3 Bake 5 minutes; cool. Reduce oven temperature to 350°F.

4 Meanwhile, in small microwavable bowl, place butter and chocolate. Microwave uncovered on High, 1 to 2 minutes, stirring every 30 seconds, until mixture can be stirred smooth; cool slightly.

5 In medium bowl, beat chocolate mixture and remaining ingredients except hazelnuts and sweetened whipped cream with electric mixer on low speed. Stir in hazelnuts. Spread in pastry-lined pan.

6 Bake 50 to 60 minutes or until set. Remove from oven and cool in pan on cooling rack 10 minutes. Without releasing sides of pan, run knife around side of pan carefully to loosen tart. Gently remove sides of pan.

7 Serve warm with whipped cream. Cover and refrigerate any remaining tart.

* To toast hazelnuts and remove skins: Heat oven to 350°F. Spread nuts in 15×10×1-inch baking pan. Bake uncovered 8 to 10 minutes, stirring occasionally, or until golden brown. Place nuts on clean dish drying towel; rub vigorously to remove skins. Discard skins.

1 Serving Calories 380; Total Fat 21g (Saturated Fat 7g, Trans Fat 0g); Cholesterol 60mg; Sodium 270mg; Total Carbohydrate 44g (Dietary Fiber 2g); Protein 5g **Carbohydrate Choices:** 3

From our 1995 *Delicious Summer Desserts* magazine, we love how the pretty colors of in-season fruit get shown off in all their glory in this easy and luscious dessert.

Summer Fruit Tart

Prep Time: 35 Minutes
Start to Finish: 2 Hours
    55 Minutes
8 servings

PECAN TART SHELL
1 cup Gold Medal
    all-purpose flour
1/2 cup finely chopped pecans
1/4 cup sugar

1/4 cup butter, softened
1 egg

FILLING AND TOPPING
1 tablespoon cold water
1 teaspoon unflavored gelatin
1/2 cup sugar
2 eggs
2 tablespoons lemon zest
1/4 cup fresh lemon juice

1/2 cup heavy whipping cream
1 cup halved strawberries
1 cup raspberries
1/2 cup blackberries or
    blueberries
1 mango or small papaya,
    peeled and sliced
1/3 cup apricot jam, melted

1 Heat oven to 375°F. Grease 9×1-inch tart pan with shortening or spray with cooking spray.

2 In medium bowl, mix 1 cup flour, the pecans, and 1/4 cup sugar. Mix in 1/4 cup butter and 1 egg until crumbly. Press in bottom and up side of pan.

3 Bake 15 to 20 minutes or until light golden brown. Cool completely.

4 Meanwhile, in 1 1/2-quart saucepan, place water. Sprinkle gelatin over water to soften; set aside. In medium bowl, beat 1/2 cup sugar and 2 eggs with electric mixer on medium speed until thick and lemon colored; stir into gelatin mixture. Heat over low heat about 15 minutes, stirring constantly, or just until boiling. Remove from heat. Stir in lemon zest and juice; set aside. In medium bowl, beat whipping cream with electric mixer on low speed, gradually increasing speed to high, until soft peaks form. Fold in lemon mixture.

5 Spread lemon mixture evenly in tart shell. Refrigerate uncovered 2 hours. Arrange fruits on filling, drizzle with jam. Cover and refrigerate any remaining tart.

1 Serving Calories 400; Total Fat 18g (Saturated Fat 8g, Trans Fat 0g); Cholesterol 100mg; Sodium 80mg; Total Carbohydrate 53g (Dietary Fiber 4g); Protein 6g **Carbohydrate Choices:** 3 1/2

The term dowdy refers to the practice of cutting the dough into pieces after it's baked, making the cozy topping dowdy looking, but absolutely delicious! This homespun American recipe mixes apples with juicy blackberries for a flavorful treat. Sprinkle with additional cinnamon and nutmeg, if you like.

Apple-Blackberry Pandowdy

Prep Time: 20 Minutes
Start to Finish: 1 Hour
20 Minutes
8 servings

FRUIT FILLING

4 medium tart cooking apples, peeled, thinly sliced (4 cups)
2 cups fresh or frozen blackberries

½ cup sugar
½ teaspoon ground cinnamon
¼ teaspoon salt
¼ teaspoon ground nutmeg
⅓ cup maple-flavored syrup or mild-flavor (light) molasses
2 tablespoons butter, melted

PASTRY

1¼ cups Gold Medal all-purpose flour
¼ teaspoon salt
⅓ cup vegetable shortening
3 to 4 tablespoons milk
3 tablespoons butter, melted
Sweetened Whipped Cream (page 227) or plain whipping cream

1 Heat oven to 350°F.

2 In large bowl, mix apples, blackberries, sugar, cinnamon, ¼ teaspoon salt, and nutmeg. In ungreased 2-quart casserole, spread fruit mixture. In small bowl, mix syrup and 2 tablespoons melted butter; pour over fruit mixture.

3 In medium bowl, mix flour and ¼ teaspoon salt. Cut in shortening, using pastry blender or fork, until mixture forms coarse crumbs the size of small peas. Sprinkle with milk, 1 tablespoon at a time, tossing with fork until all of flour is moistened and pastry almost cleans bowl side. Gather pastry into a ball. On lightly floured surface, shape into flattened round. Roll out into shape to fit top of casserole. Fit pastry over fruit mixture inside rim of casserole. Brush with 3 tablespoons melted butter. Cut slits near center with point of paring knife.

4 Bake 30 minutes. Remove from oven. Cut crust into small pieces with sharp knife, mixing pieces into fruit mixture.

5 Bake about 30 minutes longer or until apples are tender and pieces of crust are golden. Serve warm with sweetened whipped cream.

1 Serving Calories 410; Total Fat 21g (Saturated Fat 10g, Trans Fat 0.5g); Cholesterol 35mg; Sodium 220mg; Total Carbohydrate 52g (Dietary Fiber 3g); Protein 3g **Carbohydrate Choices:** 3½

We found this recipe in a 1971 Bisquick cookbook. If you find yourself with a lot of fresh blueberries on hand, we've added a version below for you!

Bar Harbor Blueberry Cobbler

Prep Time: 10 Minutes
Start to Finish: 40 Minutes
6 servings

1 can (21 oz) blueberry pie filling
1 teaspoon orange zest
1 cup Bisquick Original Pancake
& Baking Mix

¼ cup fresh orange juice
1 tablespoon sugar
1 tablespoon butter, softened
Half-and-half, if desired

1 Heat oven to 400°F.

2 In ungreased 1½-quart casserole, mix pie filling and orange zest. Bake 15 minutes.

3 Meanwhile, mix remaining ingredients except half-and-half until soft dough forms. Drop by 6 spoonfuls onto hot blueberry mixture.

4 Bake 15 to 20 minutes or until topping is light golden brown. Serve warm with half-and-half.

Fresh Blueberry Cobbler: Omit pie filling. In 2-quart saucepan, mix ½ cup sugar and 1 tablespoon cornstarch. Stir in 2 cups fresh blueberries, 2 tablespoons water, 1 teaspoon fresh orange juice, and the orange zest. Heat to boiling, stirring constantly. Boil and stir 1 minute. Pour into ungreased 1½-quart casserole (do not bake) and continue as directed in Step 3.

1 Serving Calories 210; Total Fat 3g (Saturated Fat 1.5g, Trans Fat 0g); Cholesterol 5mg; Sodium 210mg; Total Carbohydrate 45g (Dietary Fiber 1g); Protein 2g
Carbohydrate Choices: 3

Fan Memory

"A 'later-in-the evening' favorite. It was easy and quick to put together and wonderful served warm with ice cream!"
—Cindy D.

Pancakes

HAVE POSSIBILITIES!

BY *Betty Crocker*

● You can really have a whirl with pancakes. They're on demand for breakfast? Serve, too, for lunch or dinner. With sausage, etc., as "the main idea". Or with syrup, or jelly, as dessert. (I vote for old-time egg pancakes—made quick-like, with Bisquick!)

COLONIAL JELLY STACK—pancakes piled up, party-style. Shown above. Dessert, and delicious! Make six egg pancakes (simple with Bisquick). Each at least 6 inches across. Pile up, with jelly and a little softened butter between. Sprinkle confectioners' sugar over top. Cut pie-fashion. Serve hot.

To make the pancakes simply add eggs, milk, a little butter or other fat, to Bisquick. See package. Such fluffy, tender pancakes, too. With real flavor.

THERE'S SHORTENING in Bisquick! Pure vegetable shortening, blended with the other ingredients: baking powder, Gold Medal Enriched Flour, salt, sugar, powdered milk. Six ingredients in Bisquick. We mix all six to save you work. Just add milk for biscuits! My staff likes this method.

● **HOLLY-TIME SUPPER** . . .
Chicken Salad
in
Molded Cranberry Ring
Little Hot Enriched Rolls
Colonial Jelly Stack
(Made with Bisquick Pancakes)
Coffee   Milk

CHICKEN SALAD can do with a touch of crispness. Add cut-up salted almonds. Or bits of crisp bacon.

"EASY" IS RIGHT! Referring to things made with Bisquick. Muffins, biscuits, waffles, pancakes, dumplings, etc. Simple directions on pkg. . No flops! Those Bisquick ingredients are so skilfully blended.

● **VEGETABLE POTPOURRI** fairly bursts with vitamins. Tasty, too.
1½ cups cut Cabbage   ¾ tsp. Salt
1 cup sliced Carrots   2 tbsp. Salad
½ cup chopped   Oil or
    Onion   Butter
½ cup chopped   ½ cup Boiling
    Celery   Water
Combine and cook covered until tender (about 20 minutes). 4 servings.

Free! New "Menu and Shopping Guide" for point rationing. Handy reference list of rationed foods with space for point values. Space for menus. Grocery check lists. To get your pad, mail postcard today to General Mills, Inc., Dept. 496, Minneapolis 15, Minnesota.

This recipe was originally called "Peachy Custard Kuchen" when it appeared in a fall baking magazine of ours. It is an easy adaptation of a German fruit- or cheese-filled coffee cake. Whatever you call it, you'll adore the creamy, spiced flavors of this dessert.

Peachy Custard Squares

Prep Time: 15 Minutes
Start to Finish: 1 Hour
9 servings

1 cup Gold Medal
    all-purpose flour
2 tablespoons sugar
¼ teaspoon salt
⅛ teaspoon baking powder
¼ cup butter
3 medium peaches, peeled,
    sliced (1½ cups)

⅓ cup sugar
1 teaspoon ground cinnamon
2 egg yolks
1 cup heavy whipping cream
Sweetened Whipped Cream
    (page 227), if desired

1 Heat oven to 400°F.

2 In medium bowl, mix flour, 2 tablespoons sugar, the salt, and baking powder. Cut in butter, using pastry blender or fork, until mixture forms fine crumbs. Pat mixture firmly and evenly in bottom and halfway up sides of ungreased 9-inch square pan.

3 Spread peaches in crust in pan. In small bowl, mix ⅓ cup sugar and the cinnamon; sprinkle over peaches. Bake 15 minutes.

4 In medium bowl, beat egg yolks and 1 cup whipping cream with electric mixer on medium speed about 2 minutes or until smooth. Pour custard over peaches.

5 Bake 25 to 30 minutes or until custard is set and edges are light brown. Serve warm with whipped cream. Store covered in refrigerator.

Betty's Kitchen Tip: 2 cups sliced peeled tart apples or pears or ½ bag (16 oz) frozen sliced peaches, thawed and drained, can be used for the fresh peaches.

1 Serving Calories 250; Total Fat 15g (Saturated Fat 9g, Trans Fat 0g); Cholesterol 85mg; Sodium 85mg; Total Carbohydrate 27g (Dietary Fiber 1g); Protein 3g **Carbohydrate Choices:** 2

A classic English dessert, summer puddings, such as this one, were a way of using up stale bread while taking advantage of summer's juicy berry bounty. The fruit and juice of the berries soften and flavor the bread, turning it into a "pudding" of sorts that's quite delicious!

Raspberry Summer Pudding

Prep Time: 10 Minutes
Start to Finish: 24 Hours 10 Minutes
8 servings

8 to 10 slices day-old soft Italian white bread
4 cups fresh raspberries
⅔ cup sugar
1 teaspoon fresh lemon juice

Whipping cream or Sweetened Whipped Cream (page 227), if desired
Additional fresh raspberries, if desired

1 Trim crusts from bread. Arrange about three-fourths of the bread on the bottom and up sides of ungreased 1½-quart bowl, soufflé dish, or pudding mold, cutting slices to fit bowl as needed.

2 In 2-quart saucepan, heat raspberries, sugar, and lemon juice over low heat for about 5 minutes, gently stirring occasionally, or until juice forms; cool slightly.

3 Spoon raspberry mixture into bread-lined bowl, using a slotted spoon. Pour the juice evenly over raspberries and bread. Cover raspberries with a single layer of remaining bread slices, cutting to fit as necessary (if bread doesn't completely cover raspberries, use additional bread slices).

4 Place a plate that fits inside of the bowl on the bread, pressing gently. Cover plate with enough plastic wrap to touch sides of bowl. Place heavy cans on plate to weight plate down. Refrigerate at least 24 hours but no longer than 48 hours.

5 To serve, remove cans, plastic wrap, and plate. Loosen edge of pudding with thin knife or metal spatula. Invert into shallow serving dish. Serve with whipping cream and additional raspberries.

Betty's Cooking Tip: Using in-season raspberries will ensure there is enough juice to soak all of the bread.

1 Serving Calories 150; Total Fat 1g (Saturated Fat 0g, Trans Fat 0g); Cholesterol 0mg; Sodium 125mg; Total Carbohydrate 34g (Dietary Fiber 4g); Protein 2g **Carbohydrate Choices:** 2

During the '50s, basic recipes with variations were frequent advertising features. Butter Crunch was introduced in 1956 as a versatile mixture that could become a pie crust, cobbler ingredient, or a topping for sundaes, pudding, custard, or fruit.

For more ways to use it, try this yummy Butter Crunch with any of the easy variations below. You can store it in the refrigerator for at least 2 weeks or freeze up to 3 months for a quick treat anytime.

Butter Crunch Parfaits

Prep Time: 15 Minutes
Start to Finish: 1 Hour
  30 Minutes
6 parfaits

BUTTER CRUNCH

1 cup Gold Medal
  all-purpose flour

1/2 cup chopped pecans,
  walnuts, or coconut

1/2 cup butter, cut into
  small pieces

1/4 cup packed brown sugar

PARFAITS

3 cups fruit-flavored yogurt
  or pudding (any flavor)

3 cups fresh or frozen (thawed)
  raspberries, blueberries,
  or sliced strawberries

Additional fresh fruit, if desired

1 Heat oven to 400°F.

2 In medium bowl, mix all butter crunch ingredients with clean hands. Spread in ungreased 13×9-inch pan.

3 Bake 15 minutes; stir. Cool completely, about 1 hour.

4 In each of 6 parfait glasses, layer 2 tablespoons butter crunch, 1/4 cup yogurt, and 1/4 cup berries; repeat layers. Top with additional fruit.

Butter Crunch–Toffee Ice Cream: Stir 3/4 cup butter crunch and 1/4 cup milk chocolate toffee bits into 3 to 4 cups softened vanilla ice cream. Spoon into ice cream cones or serve in bowls.

Butter Crunch–Topped Cupcakes: Top any unfrosted cupcakes with whipped cream (from an aerosol can); sprinkle with crumbled butter crunch.

Butter Crunch Trail Mix: Mix 1 1/2 to 2 cups butter crunch with 2 to 3 cups of your favorite ready-to-eat breakfast cereal, 1/2 cup dried apricots or dried sweetened cranberries, and 1/2 cup salted peanuts.

1 Parfait Calories 310; Total Fat 12g (Saturated Fat 6g, Trans Fat 0g); Cholesterol 25mg; Sodium 130mg; Total Carbohydrate 43g (Dietary Fiber 5g); Protein 7g **Carbohydrate Choices:** 3

Rice pudding was a staple on many American tables for holiday gatherings. It's sweet, warm, and comforting. From our *Easy Holiday Desserts* magazine, the rich, spiced rice with dried cranberries is a real treat.

Festive Rice Pudding

Prep Time: 40 Minutes
Start to Finish: 1 Hour 35 Minutes
7 servings

1 cup water
½ cup uncooked regular long-grain white rice
2 cups half-and-half
½ cup sugar
1 teaspoon vanilla

4 eggs
½ cup sweetened dried cranberries or raisins
⅛ teaspoon ground nutmeg
⅛ teaspoon ground cinnamon

1 In 1-quart saucepan, heat water and rice to boiling, stirring occasionally. Reduce heat to low, cover, and cook 15 to 20 minutes. Do not lift cover or stir until all water is absorbed and rice is tender.

2 Heat oven to 350°F.

3 In 2-quart saucepan, heat half-and-half over low heat just until very warm (do not boil). Remove from heat.

4 In large bowl, mix sugar, vanilla, and eggs; beat well. Gradually add half-and-half; blend well. Stir in rice and cranberries. Pour into ungreased 2-quart casserole. Place casserole in 13×9-inch pan; place pan in oven. Carefully add hot water to fill pan with about 1 inch hot water.

5 Bake casserole in pan of water 30 minutes. Stir pudding. Bake an additional 15 to

20 minutes or until knife inserted in center comes out clean. Sprinkle with nutmeg and cinnamon. Serve warm or cold. Cover and store any remaining pudding in the refrigerator.

Betty's Cooking Tip: This creamy pudding is a great way to use up cooked rice or when making rice, make extra. You'll need 1½ cups cooked rice for this recipe.

1 Serving Calories 280; Total Fat 11g (Saturated Fat 6g, Trans Fat 0g); Cholesterol 130mg; Sodium 80mg; Total Carbohydrate 39g (Dietary Fiber 0g); Protein 7g
Carbohydrate Choices: 2½

Fan Memory

"My mother always made this rice pudding around the holidays. I could never find a recipe for it. It was baked rice pudding . . . with a custard on top. It was so delicious and so special, I wish I could make it again."

—John-Na H.

We find this 1962 French Vanilla cake mix package, with its French words, really charming.

1 LB. 2.8 OZ. NET WT.

Betty Crocker®

French Vanilla

ARTIFICIAL FLAVOR

CAKE MIX

Magnifique!

ADD FRESH EGGS

Cheesecake used to be on practically every restaurant dessert menu in the 1980s and 1990s. No-bake desserts like this one are perfect to share with family or friends on hot summer days.

Swirls of Strawberry Lemon Cheesecake

Prep Time: 30 Minutes
Start to Finish: 4 Hours 30 Minutes
12 servings

CHEESECAKE
1 envelope unflavored gelatin
2/3 cup cold water
1/3 cup fresh lemon juice

1½ packages (8 oz each) cream cheese, softened
½ cup sour cream
½ cup sugar
1 teaspoon lemon zest

GRAHAM CRACKER CRUST
1½ cups finely crushed regular graham cracker crumbs (about 24 squares)

1/3 cup butter, melted
3 tablespoons sugar

FILLING
1 envelope unflavored gelatin
¼ cup cold water
1 cup frozen (thawed) strawberries with sugar (do not drain; from 15-oz container)

1 Heat oven to 350°F.

2 In 1-quart saucepan, sprinkle 1 envelope gelatin over 2/3 cup cold water; let stand 1 minute. Cook over low heat 2 to 3 minutes, stirring frequently, or until gelatin is dissolved. Remove from heat; stir in lemon juice.

3 In large bowl, beat together cream cheese, sour cream, ½ cup sugar, and lemon zest until well blended. Stir in gelatin mixture; mix well. Refrigerate 1 hour or until cream cheese mixture is the consistency of egg whites, stirring occasionally.

4 Meanwhile, in medium bowl, stir graham cracker crumbs, melted butter, and 3 tablespoons sugar. Press mixture firmly and evenly against bottom and sides of 9-inch pie plate.

5 Bake 10 minutes or until light brown. Cool on cooling rack 30 minutes.

6 In 1-quart saucepan, sprinkle 1 envelope gelatin over ¼ cup cold water; let stand 1 minute. Cook over low heat 1 to 2 minutes, stirring frequently, or until gelatin is dissolved. Remove from heat. Stir in strawberries and juice; mix well. Refrigerate 20 minutes or until mixture mounds slightly when dropped from a spoon.

7 To assemble cheesecake, pour half of the cream cheese mixture into crust. Pour strawberry filling over cream cheese mixture; top with remaining cream cheese mixture. Pull knife through all layers of filling to swirl strawberry filling throughout cream cheese mixture. Refrigerate uncovered at least 3 hours or overnight. Cover and store any remaining cheesecake in refrigerator.

1 Serving Calories 290; Total Fat 18g (Saturated Fat 10g, Trans Fat 0.5g); Cholesterol 50mg; Sodium 190mg; Total Carbohydrate 28g (Dietary Fiber 0g); Protein 4g **Carbohydrate Choices:** 2

Taken from the *Betty Crocker's Buffets* cookbook (1984), this meringue torte is tall and light, with billowy whipped cream and fresh fruit between layers of baked meringue. It's a great option after a heavy meal or any time you're looking for a dessert that's not too filling.

Strawberry-Meringue Torte

Prep Time: 25 Minutes
Start to Finish: 3 Hours 25 Minutes
12 servings

4 egg whites
¼ teaspoon cream of tartar
½ teaspoon almond extract
1¼ cups sugar
1½ cups heavy whipping cream

1½ cups sliced fresh strawberries
Additional whole or halved strawberries, if desired
Mint leaves, if desired

1 Heat oven to 225°F. Line cookie sheet with cooking parchment paper. Draw two 8-inch circles on paper.

2 In medium bowl, beat egg whites and cream of tartar with electric mixer on low speed until thickened. Gradually increase speed to high, beating until foamy. Beat in almond extract. Gradually beat in 1 cup sugar, about 1 tablespoon at a time; continue beating until stiff and glossy. Divide meringue evenly between the 2 circles; spread to fill each circle.

3 Bake 1½ hours. Turn off oven; leave meringues in oven 1 hour with door closed. Finish cooling meringues at room temperature.

4 In small bowl, beat whipping cream and ¼ cup sugar with electric mixer on low speed until thickened. Gradually increase speed to high, beating until stiff peaks form.

5 Place 1 meringue on serving plate; spread with 1½ cups whipped cream. Arrange sliced strawberries on whipped cream. Place second meringue on top of strawberries. Spread with remaining whipped cream. Garnish with additional strawberries and mint leaves. Cover and refrigerate any remaining torte.

Make-Ahead Directions: After Step 3, wrap and freeze meringues up to 1 week. Let stand at room temperature 30 minutes before assembling the dessert.

1 Serving Calories 190; Total Fat 9g (Saturated Fat 6g, Trans Fat 0g); Cholesterol 35mg; Sodium 30mg; Total Carbohydrate 23g (Dietary Fiber 0g); Protein 2g **Carbohydrate Choices:** 1½

Shortcakes are rich biscuits, usually filled with whipped cream and fresh berries. We have created over 300 recipes for shortcake, which are now in our recipe database. We shouldn't have a favorite, but this Bisquick recipe with coconut, filled with assorted berries and whipped cream, rises to the top of our list.

Coconut Biscuit Shortcakes

Prep Time: 30 Minutes
Start to Finish: 45 Minutes
6 shortcakes

2⅓ cups Bisquick Original Pancake & Baking Mix
¾ cup coconut, lightly toasted*
½ cup milk
4 tablespoons sugar
3 tablespoons butter, melted

½ teaspoon ground cinnamon
1 quart (4 cups) assorted fresh berries
Sweetened Whipped Cream (page 227)
1 tablespoon chopped fresh mint, if desired

1 Heat oven to 425°F.

2 In large bowl, mix Bisquick mix, coconut, milk, 3 tablespoons of the sugar, the butter, and cinnamon until soft dough forms. Turn dough onto surface dusted with Bisquick mix. Shape into ball; knead 8 to 10 times. Roll dough ½ inch thick. Sprinkle with remaining 1 tablespoon sugar. With 3-inch biscuit cutter dipped in Bisquick mix, cut into 6 shortcakes, rerolling scraps as necessary. Place on ungreased cookie sheet.

3 Bake 10 to 12 minutes or until golden brown. Split warm shortcakes in half horizontally. Fill with berries and whipped cream; sprinkle with mint.

* To toast coconut: Heat oven to 350°F. Spread coconut in ungreased shallow pan. Bake uncovered 5 to 7 minutes, stirring occasionally, until golden brown.

1 Shortcake Calories 410; Total Fat 13g (Saturated Fat 8g, Trans Fat 0g); Cholesterol 25mg; Sodium 550mg; Total Carbohydrate 68g (Dietary Fiber 5g); Protein 6g
Carbohydrate Choices: 4½

Betty Crocker staff, 1934.

The delicious flavors and textures of this dessert from *Betty Crocker's Old-Fashioned Desserts* cookbook will wow your guests with a comforting treat. If you like, take some of the pressure off the prep of your meal by following the make-ahead directions below.

Pear-Fig Strudel with Eggnog Sauce

Prep Time: 25 Minutes
Start to Finish: 1 Hour
10 servings

STRUDEL

2 lb ripe pears, peeled, coarsely
   chopped
1 teaspoon lemon zest
2 tablespoons fresh lemon juice

½ cup pistachio nuts, coarsely
   chopped
⅓ to ½ cup granulated sugar
½ teaspoon ground cinnamon
¼ teaspoon ground ginger
¼ teaspoon ground cloves
8 oz dried figs, stems removed,
   cut in half (from 10-oz bag)
⅓ cup plain dry bread crumbs

6 sheets frozen phyllo (filo)
   pastry (18×14 inch), thawed
½ cup butter, melted
Powdered sugar, if desired

EGGNOG SAUCE

2 cups dairy eggnog
1 tablespoon cornstarch

1 In 12-inch skillet, mix pears, lemon zest, and lemon juice. Heat over medium heat about 5 minutes, stirring occasionally, or until pears are soft; remove from heat. Stir in pistachio nuts, granulated sugar, cinnamon, ginger, cloves, and figs; mix well. Stir in bread crumbs; set aside.

2 Heat oven to 400°F.

3 Line 15×10×1-inch pan with cooking parchment paper or aluminum foil. Place phyllo sheets on work surface, cover with clean damp towel. Working with one sheet at a time, brush with melted butter; fold lengthwise in half. Brush top with butter. Repeat with remaining sheets; stack sheets on top of one another; place on damp towel. Spoon pear mixture on dough to within 2 inches from edges. Fold sides over pear mixture. Starting at long edge near filling, roll up using towel to help roll. Place seam side down diagonally in pan. Brush with butter.

4 Bake about 30 minutes, brushing with butter every 10 minutes, or until golden brown.

5 Meanwhile, in 2-quart saucepan, mix eggnog and cornstarch with whisk. Heat over medium heat, stirring constantly, until boiling. Boil and stir 1 minute or until slightly thickened. Cover and let stand at room temperature while strudel bakes.

6 Cool strudel slightly; dust with powdered sugar. With serrated knife, cut into 10 slices. Serve warm with eggnog sauce.

Make-Ahead Directions: After preparing eggnog sauce, cover and refrigerate. Cover and refrigerate unbaked strudel up to 24 hours

before baking. Bake as directed. Sauce can be served cold or warm. To heat, place sauce in 1-quart saucepan. Heat over medium-low heat, stirring frequently, just until heated through.

1 Serving Calories 400; Total Fat 16g (Saturated Fat 9g, Trans Fat 0g); Cholesterol 50mg; Sodium 210mg; Total Carbohydrate 56g (Dietary Fiber 6g); Protein 5g **Carbohydrate Choices:** 4

An irresistible combination of whipped cream paired with fresh fruit at its peak of flavor, fools have been enjoyed in England since the 16th century. This recipe, buried deep in our cookbook archives, is one to keep on hand for a really simple yet sensational summer dessert when berries are at their peak of flavor.

Strawberry-Raspberry Fool

Prep Time: 10 Minutes
Start to Finish: 2 Hours
   10 Minutes
4 servings

1 cup sliced fresh strawberries
1 cup fresh raspberries
⅓ cup plus ¼ cup powdered
   sugar

1½ cups heavy whipping cream
Additional berries and fresh
   mint leaves, if desired

1 In blender, place strawberries, raspberries, and ⅓ cup of the powdered sugar. Cover; blend on medium speed, stopping occasionally and scraping down sides with rubber spatula, about 1 minute. Press fruit mixture gently through fine-mesh strainer into small bowl; discard seeds.

2 In medium bowl, beat whipping cream and remaining ¼ cup powdered sugar with electric mixer on low speed until thickened. Gradually increase speed to high, beating until stiff peaks form. Fold in strained fruit mixture. Spoon into serving dishes.

3 Cover and refrigerate at least 2 hours or until chilled. Garnish with additional berries and mint leaves.

1 Serving Calories 370; Total Fat 28g (Saturated Fat 17g, Trans Fat 1g); Cholesterol 100mg; Sodium 30mg; Total Carbohydrate 27g (Dietary Fiber 3g); Protein 2g **Carbohydrate Choices:** 2

Metric Conversion Guide

Volume

US Units	Canadian Metric	Australian Metric	UK Metric
⅛ teaspoon	1 mL	1 ml	1 ml
½ teaspoon	2 mL	2 ml	2.5 ml
1 teaspoon	5 mL	5 ml	5 ml
1 tablespoon	15 mL	20 ml	15 ml
¼ cup	50 mL	60 ml	60 ml
⅓ cup	75 mL	80 ml	80 ml
½ cup	125 mL	125 ml	125 ml
⅔ cup	150 mL	170 ml	150 ml
¾ cup	175 mL	190 ml	175 ml
1 cup	250 mL	250 ml	250 ml
1 quart	1 liter	1 liter	1 liter
1½ quarts	1.5 liters	1.5 liters	1.5 liters
½ gallon (2 quarts)	2 liters	2 liters	2 liters
2½ quarts	2.5 liters	2.5 liters	2.5 liters
3 quarts	3 liters	3 liters	3 liters
1 gallon (4 quarts)	4 liters	4 liters	4 liters

Weight

US Units	Canadian Metric	Australian Metric	UK Metric
1 ounce	30 grams	30 grams	25 grams
2 ounces	55 grams	60 grams	55 grams
3 ounces	85 grams	90 grams	85 grams
4 ounces (¼ pound)	115 grams	115 grams	115 grams
8 ounces (½ pound)	225 grams	225 grams	225 grams
16 ounces (1 pound)	455 grams	450 grams	450 grams

Index

Note: Page references in *italics* indicate photographs.

A
Almond(s)
  Cardamom Cookies, *176*, 177
  -Cherry Macaroons, 184, *185*
  Dream Bars, 187
  -Filled Crescents, 38–40, *39*
  -Raspberry Crepes, 12–13, *13*
  Tipsy Squire, 41–42, *43*
Apple
  -Blackberry Pandowdy, 234, *235*
  -Raisin Bread, 122

B
Banana–Zucchini–Chocolate Chip Cake, *200*, 201
Barley-Chicken Stew with Cheddar Dumplings, 50, *51*
Bars
  Chocolate-Almond-Toffee Triangles, 190, *191*
  Coconut Chews, 188, *189*
  Dream, 187
  No-Bake Fudge Meltaways, 194, *195*
  Nutty Marshmallow, *36*, 37
  Strawberry Cheesecake, 193
  Walnut-Cinnamon Crisps, 196, *197*
  Walnut-Orange, 186
Bean(s)
  Everyday Cassoulet, 109
  Three, and Cornbread Casserole, 108
Beef
  Baked Chimichangas, 76, *77*
  Brisket, Barbecue, 87
  Burgundy, 88

Cheeseburger Deep-Dish Pizza, 75
  Crazy Crust Pizza, 74
  Italian Bake, 86
  Italian-Style Spaghetti, 81
  Parmesan Chicken-Fried Steak, 90
  Roast, Peppered, with Horseradish Sauce, 22, *23*
  Salsa Meat Loaf, *84*, 85
  Sauerbraten Meatballs and Noodles, 78, *79*
  Sweet-and-Sour Meatballs, 82, *83*
Beer Bread, 152
Berries. *See also specific berries*
  Butter Crunch Parfaits, 240, *241*
  Coconut Biscuit Shortcakes, 248, *249*
Biscuit(s)
  Bisquick Pumpkin, 138, *139*
  and Chicken, Oven-Baked, 71–72
  Maple-Pecan, *136*, 137
  Shortcakes, Coconut, 248, *249*
Blackberry-Apple Pandowdy, 234, *235*
Blueberry(ies)
  Cobbler, Bar Harbor, 236
  -Orange Pancakes, 8, *9*
  -Pineapple Buckle, 128
Brandy-Walnut Balls, No-Bake, *34*, 35
Bread Bowls, Parmesan, 154, *155*
Bread puddings
  Eggnog French Toast Strata with Cranberry Syrup, *10*, 11
  Raspberry Summer Pudding, 239
Breads. *See also* Biscuit(s); Buns; Rolls
  Apple-Raisin, 122

Beer, 152
  Cheesy Breadsticks, 150
  Chile Pepper–Cheese, No-Knead, 148, *149*
  Eggnog–Poppy Seed, *28*, 29
  Gumdrop, 30–31, *31*
  Luscious Lemon Loaf, *124*, 125
  Toffee-Orange, 126, *127*
Buns
  Magic Cinnamon Balloon, *144*, 145
  Snowman, 26, *27*
Butter Crunch Parfaits, 240, *241*
Butterscotch-Walnut Sugar Cookies, 173

C
Cakes
  Black Forest Cherry Torte, 218–19
  Blueberry-Pineapple Buckle, 128
  Bonnie Butter, 214, *215*
  Chocolate Buttermallow, 216–17
  Chocolate Nesselrode, 44–45
  Cream Cheese Pound, 203
  Fresh Strawberry-Pudding Poke, 206–8, *207*
  Lemon–Poppy Seed Pound, 210, *211*
  Raspberry and Cream Cheese Coffee Rounds, 14–16, *15*
  Raspberry-Chocolate Coffee, 140, *141*
  Spice Chiffon, 212–13
  Tipsy Squire, 41–42, *43*
  Williamsburg Orange, 204, *205*
  Zucchini–Chocolate Chip–Banana, *200*, 201
Cardamom Cookies, *176*, 177

Cassoulet, Everyday, 109
Cheese. *See also* Cream Cheese
  Cheeseburger Deep-Dish
    Pizza, 75
  Cheesy Breadsticks, 150
  –Chile Pepper Bread, No-
    Knead, 148, *149*
  Crazy Crust Pizza, 74
  Easy Chicken Lasagna, *54*, 55
  Family-Size Tuna Melt,
    102, *103*
  Ham and Egg Brunch Bake, 17
  Impossibly Easy Chicken
    Parmigiana Pie, *58*, 59
  Individual Barbecue Chicken
    Pizzas, 56
  Italian Bake, 86
  Muffuletta Sandwich, 96, *97*
  Parmesan Bread Bowls, 154, *155*
  Parmesan Chicken-Fried
    Steak, 90
Cheesecake, Swirls of
    Strawberry Lemon, 244, *245*
Cherry
  -Almond Macaroons, 184, *185*
  Cookies, Soft, 182, *183*
  -Oatmeal Muffins, *112*, 113
  Torte, Black Forest, 218–19
Chicken
  Barbecue, Pizzas,
    Individual, 56
  Barbecued, Chinese-
    Inspired, 63
  -Barley Stew with Cheddar
    Dumplings, 50, *51*
  and Biscuits, Oven-Baked,
    71–72
  Coconut, with Chutney, *20*, 21
  –Fresh Berry Salad, 60, *61*
  Hush Puppy–Fried, 68–70, *69*
  Lasagna, Easy, *54*, 55
  Lemonade Ginger, 73
  Macaroni Salad, 64, *65*
  Parmigiana Pie, Impossibly
    Easy, *58*, 59
  Salad Log, 6, *7*
  Stew, Hearty, 53

  with Wild Rice and Cranberry
    Stuffing, 66–67
Chimichangas, Baked, 76, *77*
Chocolate
  Almond-Cherry Macaroons,
    184, *185*
  -Almond-Toffee Triangles,
    190, *191*
  Black Forest Cherry Torte,
    218–19
  Bonnie Butter Cake, 214, *215*
  Buttermallow Cake, 216–17
  Chip Scones, 134
  Chip–Zucchini–Banana Cake,
    200, 201
  Cookie Muffins, *116*, 117
  -Hazelnut Tart, 230–31
  Nesselrode Cake, 44–45
  No-Bake Brandy-Walnut Balls,
    34, 35
  No-Bake Fudge Meltaways,
    194, *195*
  Peppermint Cookie Twists,
    180–81
  Pink Peppermint Pie, *46*, 47
  -Raspberry Coffee Cake,
    140, *141*
  Walnut-Orange Bars, 186
Cinnamon
  Balloon Buns, Magic, *144*,
    145
  Butterfly Rolls, 146, *147*
  -Walnut Crisps, 196, *197*
Cobbler, Bar Harbor
    Blueberry, 236
Coconut
  Biscuit Shortcakes, 248, *249*
  Chews, 188, *189*
  Chicken with Chutney, *20*, 21
  Dream Bars, 187
  No-Bake Fudge Meltaways,
    194, *195*
Coffee Cake
  Raspberry and Cream Cheese
    Coffee Rounds, 14–16, *15*
  Raspberry-Chocolate, 140,
    141

Cookies. *See also* Bars
  Almond-Cherry Macaroons,
    184, *185*
  Almond-Filled Crescents,
    38–40, *39*
  Butterscotch-Walnut Sugar,
    173
  Cardamom, *176*, 177
  Cherry, Soft, 182, *183*
  Chocolate Peppermint Cookie
    Twists, 180–81
  Christmas Jewels, 32, *33*
  Date Pinwheels, 178, *179*
  Fruit-Slice, 169–70, *171*
  Ginger Creams, *174*, 175
  Lemon-Ginger Crinkles,
    158, 159
  Lemon-Hazelnut, 162, *163*
  No-Bake Brandy-Walnut Balls,
    34, 35
  Oatmeal Refrigerator, 172
  Pineapple, 161
  Salted Peanut Crisps, 166, *167*
  Spiced Pumpkin-Date, 164
  Vanilla Crispies, 168
Cornbread and Three Bean
    Casserole, 108
Corn-Oatmeal Muffins, 120, *121*
Cranberry(ies)
  Festive Rice Pudding, 242
  Orange Streusel Muffins, 115
  Syrup, Eggnog French Toast
    Strata with, *10*, 11
  and Wild Rice Stuffing,
    Chicken with, 66–67
Cream, Sweetened
    Whipped, 227
Cream Cheese
  Chicken Salad Log, 6, *7*
  Pineapple Cheese Ball, 2, *3*
  Pound Cake, 203
  and Raspberry Coffee Rounds,
    14–16, *15*
  Strawberry Cheesecake
    Bars, 193
  Swirls of Strawberry Lemon
    Cheesecake, 244, *245*

Crepes, Raspberry-Almond, 12–13, *13*
Currant(s)
 -Lemon Scones, *132*, 133
 Snowman Buns, 26, *27*

D

Date
 Pinwheels, 178, *179*
 -Pumpkin Cookies, Spiced, 164
Dip, Green Goddess, 5

E

Egg and Ham Brunch Bake, 17
Eggnog
 French Toast Strata with Cranberry Syrup, *10*, 11
 –Poppy Seed Bread, *28*, 29
 Sauce, Pear-Fig Strudel with, 250–51, *251*

F

Fig-Pear Strudel with Eggnog Sauce, 250–51, *251*
Fish. *See* Tuna Melt
Franks in a Loaf, Mexican-Style, 98
Fruit. *See also specific fruits*
 Chocolate Nesselrode Cake, 44–45
 Christmas Jewels, 32, *33*
 Summer, Tart, *232*, 233
 Tropical, Salad, Creamy, 18–19, *19*

G

Ginger
 Creams, *174*, 175
 Lemonade Chicken, 73
 -Lemon Crinkles, *158*, 159
 Green Goddess Dip, 5
 Gumdrop Bread, 30–31, *31*

H

Ham
 and Egg Brunch Bake, 17
 Muffuletta Sandwich, 96, *97*

Hazelnut
 -Chocolate Tart, 230–31
 -Lemon Cookies, 162, *163*
Honey Orange Muffins, 118, *119*
Horseradish Sauce, Peppered Beef Roast with, 22, *23*
Hot dogs. *See* Franks

L

Lasagna, Easy Chicken, *54*, 55
Lemon
 Cheesecake, Swirls of Strawberry, 244, *245*
 -Currant Scones, *132*, 133
 -Ginger Crinkles, *158*, 159
 -Hazelnut Cookies, 162, *163*
 Loaf, Luscious, *124*, 125
 –Poppy Seed Pound Cake, 210, *211*
Lemonade Ginger Chicken, 73

M

Macaroons, Almond-Cherry, 184, *185*
Maple-Pecan Biscuits, *136*, 137
Marshmallow creme
 Chocolate Buttermallow Cake, 216–17
 Nutty Marshmallow Bars, 36, 37
Marshmallows
 Magic Cinnamon Balloon Buns, *144*, 145
 Pink Peppermint Pie, *46*, 47
Meatballs
 Sauerbraten, and Noodles, 78, *79*
 Sweet-and-Sour, 82, *83*
Meat Loaf, Salsa, *84*, 85
Meringue
 Rhubarb-, Squares, *228*, 229
 Strawberry-, Torte, 246, *247*
Muffins
 Chocolate Cookie, *116*, 117
 Corn-Oatmeal, 120, *121*
 Cranberry Orange Streusel, 115
 Oatmeal-Cherry, *112*, 113

Orange Honey, 118, *119*
Muffuletta Sandwich, 96, *97*
Mushrooms
 Beef Burgundy, 88
 Crazy Crust Pizza, 74
 Italian Bake, 86
 Pork Chop and New Potato Skillet, *94*, 95

N

Noodles
 Hearty Chicken Stew, 53
 Sauerbraten Meatballs and, 78, *79*
Nuts. *See also specific nuts*
 Christmas Jewels, 32, *33*

O

Oats
 Corn-Oatmeal Muffins, 120, *121*
 Oatmeal-Cherry Muffins, *112*, 113
 Oatmeal Refrigerator Cookies, 172
Olives
 Muffuletta Sandwich, 96, *97*
Orange
 Cake, Williamsburg, 204, *205*
 Cranberry Streusel Muffins, 115
 Honey Muffins, 118, *119*
 -Toffee Bread, 126, *127*
 -Walnut Bars, 186

P

Pancakes
 Blueberry-Orange, 8, *9*
 Buttermilk, Fluffy, 130, *131*
Papaya Salsa–Grilled Pork Tacos, 92–93, *93*
Parfaits, Butter Crunch, 240, *241*
Pasta. *See also* Noodles
 Chicken Macaroni Salad, 64, *65*
 Creamy Tropical Fruit Salad, 18–19, *19*
 Easy Chicken Lasagna, *54*, 55
 Italian-Style Spaghetti, 81

Ravioli with Roasted Red Pepper Cream, 106, *107*
Rigatoni–Smoked Bratwurst Skillet, 91
Seafood Salad with Ginger Dressing, *104*, 105
Peach(es)
'n' Cream Pie, Impossibly Easy, 226
Oven-Baked Chicken and Biscuits, 71–72
Peachy Custard Squares, 238
Pie, Blushing, *220*, 221
Peanut(s)
Crisps, Salted, 166, *167*
Nutty Marshmallow Bars, *36*, 37
Pear-Fig Strudel with Eggnog Sauce, 250–51, *251*
Pecan(s)
Butter Crunch Parfaits, 240, *241*
-Maple Biscuits, *136*, 137
Peppermint
Chocolate Cookie Twists, 180–81
Pie, Pink, *46*, 47
Pepper(s)
Chile, –Cheese Bread, No-Knead, 148, *149*
Roasted Red, Cream, Ravioli with, 106, *107*
Sweet-and-Sour Meatballs, 82, *83*
Pie Pastry, 222
Pies
Blushing Peach, *220*, 221
Chicken Parmigiana, Impossibly Easy, *58*, 59
One-Crust, Baked, 223
One-Crust, Partially Baked, 223
Peaches 'n' Cream, Impossibly Easy, 226
Pink Peppermint, *46*, 47
Shaker Sugar, *224*, 225

Pineapple
-Blueberry Buckle, 128
Cheese Ball, 2, *3*
Cookies, 161
Creamy Tropical Fruit Salad, 18–19, *19*
Gumdrop Bread, 30–31, *31*
Sweet-and-Sour Meatballs, 82, *83*
Pizzas
Barbecue Chicken, Individual, 56
Cheeseburger Deep-Dish, 75
Crazy Crust, 74
Poppy Seed
–Eggnog Bread, *28*, 29
–Lemon Pound Cake, 210, *211*
Pork. *See also* Ham; Sausages
Chop and New Potato Skillet, *94*, 95
Grilled, –Papaya Salsa Tacos, 92–93, *93*
Roast, Savory, 24
Sauerbraten Meatballs and Noodles, 78, *79*
Potato, New, and Pork Chop Skillet, *94*, 95
Pudding
Festive Rice, 242
Raspberry Summer, 239
Pumpkin
Biscuits, Bisquick, 138, *139*
-Date Cookies, Spiced, 164

R
Raisin(s)
-Apple Bread, 122
Williamsburg Orange Cake, 204, *205*
Raspberry(ies)
-Almond Crepes, 12–13, *13*
-Chocolate Coffee Cake, 140, *141*
and Cream Cheese Coffee Rounds, 14–16, *15*
Fresh Berry–Chicken Salad, 60, *61*

-Strawberry Fool, 252
Summer Fruit Tart, *232*, 233
Summer Pudding, 239
Rhubarb-Meringue Squares, *228*, 229
Rice
Pudding, Festive, 242
Wild, and Cranberry Stuffing, Chicken with, 66–67
Rolls
Butterfly, 146, *147*
Cloverleaf, 143
Crescent, 143
Fan Tan, 143
Four-Leaf-Clover, 143
Refrigerator Roll Dough, 142

S
Salads
Chicken Macaroni, 64, *65*
Fresh Berry–Chicken, 60, *61*
Pasta Seafood, with Ginger Dressing, *104*, 105
Tropical Fruit, Creamy, 18–19, *19*
Salsa Meat Loaf, *84*, 85
Sandwiches
Family-Size Tuna Melt, 102, *103*
Muffuletta, 96, *97*
Sauce, Sherry Custard, 41, *43*
Sauerbraten Meatballs and Noodles, 78, *79*
Sausages
Everyday Cassoulet, 109
Muffuletta Sandwich, 96, *97*
Rigatoni–Smoked Bratwurst Skillet, 91
Scones
Chocolate Chip, 134
Lemon-Currant, *132*, 133
Seafood
Family-Size Tuna Melt, 102, *103*
Margarita Shrimp, 99, *100*
Pasta Seafood Salad with Ginger Dressing, *104*, 105

Shaker Sugar Pie, *224*, 225
Sherry Custard Sauce, 41, *43*
Shortcakes, Coconut Biscuit,
    248, *249*
Shrimp
  Margarita, 99, *100*
  Pasta Seafood Salad with
    Ginger Dressing, *104*, 105
Snowman Buns, 26, *27*
Spice Chiffon Cake, 212–13
Spreads
  Chicken Salad Log, 6, *7*
  Pineapple Cheese Ball, 2, *3*
Squash. *See* Pumpkin; Zucchini
Stews
  Beef Burgundy, 88
  Chicken, Hearty, 53
  Chicken-Barley, with Cheddar
    Dumplings, 50, *51*
Strawberry(ies)
  Cheesecake Bars, 193
  Fresh Berry–Chicken Salad,
    60, *61*
  -Meringue Torte, 246, *247*
  -Pudding Poke Cake, Fresh,
    206–8, *207*
  -Raspberry Fool, 252
  Summer Fruit Tart, *232*, 233
  Swirls of, Lemon Cheesecake,
    244, *245*
Strudel, Pear-Fig, with Eggnog
    Sauce, 250–51, *251*

T

Tacos, Grilled Pork–Papaya
    Salsa, 92–93, *93*
Tarts
  Chocolate-Hazelnut, 230–31
  Summer Fruit, *232*, 233
Tipsy Squire, 41–42, *43*
Toffee
  -Almond-Chocolate Triangles,
    190, *191*
  -Orange Bread, 126, *127*
Tortillas
  Baked Chimichangas, 76, *77*
  Grilled Pork–Papaya Salsa
    Tacos, 92–93, *93*
Tuna Melt, Family-Size, 102, *103*

V

Vanilla Crispies, 168

W

Walnut(s)
  -Brandy Balls, No-Bake, *34*, 35
  -Butterscotch Sugar
    Cookies, 173
  -Cinnamon Crisps, 196, *197*
  Coconut Chews, 188, *189*
  -Orange Bars, 186
Whipped Cream,
    Sweetened, 227
Wild Rice and Cranberry
    Stuffing, Chicken with,
    66–67

Y

Yogurt
  Butter Crunch Parfaits,
    240, *241*

Z

Zucchini–Chocolate Chip–
    Banana Cake, *200*, 201

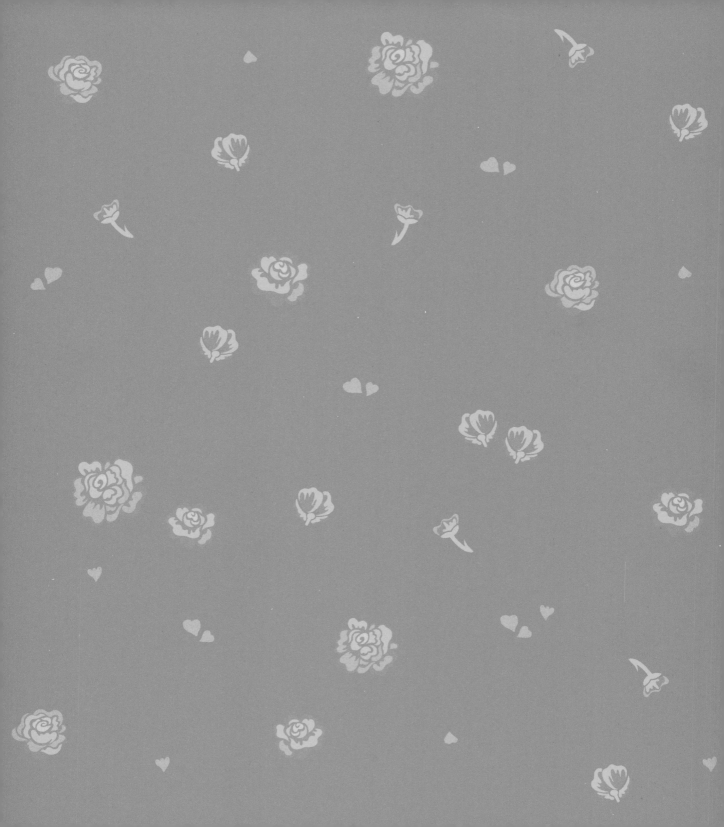